CLOTH OF THE TEMPEST

BOOKS BY KENNETH PATCHEN

Poetry:

AN ASTONISHED EYE LOOKS OUT OF THE AIR
THE DARK KINGDOM
SELECTED POEMS
BEFORE THE BRAVE
THE TEETH OF THE LION
FIRST WILL & TESTAMENT
PICTURES OF LIFE AND OF DEATH
CLOTH OF THE TEMPEST

Prose:

SLEEPERS AWAKE
MEMOIRS OF A SHY PORNOGRAPHER
THEY KEEP RIDING DOWN ALL THE TIME
SEE YOU IN THE MORNING
THE JOURNAL OF ALBION MOONLIGHT

Prose-Poetry:

PANELS FOR THE WALLS OF HEAVEN

AWAITING PUBLICATION

Prose:

I WONDER WHAT EVER BECAME OF HUMAN BEINGS
THE HUMAN WINTER
THE SURRENDER OF THE WORLD

Prose-Poetry:

THE STORY OF JEREMIAH DORK AND THE KILADIAN FOREST
INSCRIPTIONS FOR THE DARK ROOMS OF THIS WORLD

Poetry:

ANGEL & MONSTER

CLOTH OF THE TEMPEST

TEMPEST

KENNETH PATCHEN

PUBLISHED BY
PADELL
830 BROADWAY
NEW YORK

This, the second edition, consists of 2500 copies.
—March 1948

PRINTED IN THE UNITED STATES OF AMERICA
BY GANIS AND HARRIS, NEW YORK

for Miriam

White lions of snow
stare sleepily down
from the roofs of the
village, as I leave
the darkening wood.
The lights are just com-
ing on — Christ!
everything looks so
pure and safe! I can
smell suppers cook-
ing. Somewhere a
frosty bell starts to
ring. The evening

star is coming out
as I turn in at

the gate. It looks
cold and silent in
the waiting sky.
She opens the door
and I take her into
my arms. Her mouth
feels very warm
against my cold one.
"What did you see

in the *woods today?" There is a
faint smell of buttery cinnamon in
her hair. "Oh, nothing very special—
maybe a tiny little deer, just about big
enough to walk ••• over by the old
barn…" +"Oh, you're mean to tease
! tell me mmm was it terribly
pretty !! I press my lips
into the soft hollow of her
throat. "Not half as
pretty As you* are, I
Manage to tell her. —Out in
the world it is
quite dark now.

JANUARY 1948

THE CHILDHOOD OF GOD

Ball. Bell. Green. Blue. Run. Do.
Curly. Warm. Nest. Round. Laugh.
Goat. Lamb. Kitten. Bird.
Dark. Sleep.

Arms. Milk. Legs. Water. Seven.
Wall. Sea. Blade. Push. Coax.
Dry. Sun. Wind. Door. Fountain.
All.

Fawn. Burn. Tide. Spear. Flood.
Hair. Tear.

Scar. Fly. Blood.
Flow.

Slay. Vine. Grove.
Field.

Where?
Sleep.
Body. Gold. Moving.

MONSTER ON A YELLOW MORNING

foot

eat

foot

eat

WORLD

foot

world

Eat

eat

foot

yellowing

eat

THE CREATION

rock
silt
fish
WATER

wind
star
leaf
moon

FISHWHELPS

crawl
break
lance

windflaming

rot
see
fly

Beastgod

womb
grow
burn

3

THE ANCESTRAL CREATURE

Night festers in the cave
Of his phantomshaded fancyhood . . .
Covered with thick hair,
Gnawing the bone of a serid-ox—
What did he fear?
Was there a yellow animal
In the mud of his wordlessness?
How did he think?
Did the . . . and tusks . . . furred stink . . .
The dismal green towers . . . ICE . . . pain . . .
Hoofs and the leaf . . . to bite . . . shinetiger . . .
Grasseyed on the battlemented ground . . .

Cried

All in the foaming
The bloodstilled thrones of that wilderness . . .

And thick over his sight
The eye of fire
Rending the finclotted heavens . . .

Farther going. Swim. Kill. Run. Die.

CRUELTIES OF THE SPORTIVE POWER

Loved in the black weather . . . The

Will. Life's gay will. The will of
Life. Sea. Joy. Bird. Queen. Flame.
Beast.
Stain.
The will of life. Stain on the golden
Throat.   And life's wit
On the mountain. My chair. My tree. My
Lady.
And the will and the wit of the flaming bird
And the way and the wiles of the seaqueen child
And the word and the warmth of life's
Golden wakening

My tongue head cry juice great and small
Of life. Chair star tree. My
Sound lady. All in the golden weather
Of my love. Near the beast.
Please be wandering. Taste of flame
In my mouth. Green brain of His being.
Deeper to holy. Like an iron bull in a cloud.

VISION OF THE EXACT GRACE

As O in the green will . . .
Serpent at the gate . . . (This is the word.) Fallen
As *this angel*!

Milk to nourish God.

Appoint another . . . O every forest wills an angel. On pale lake
Skates death's white kids. Man is. As O in my world
The serpent laughs.

Angel! Angel! *in light*

This is the gate. O each meadow frogs the black and swollen fly . . .
In broachplay this clever sun. Legs of the wind buckle sleepily
Over hills and the great towns. Life is! As O in my glee
The beautiful weeps.

Approve this other . . . O every man trees in his own place. My God
Withers in the fire O in the cold fire that pours down
From a sky of blood

As O in my heart the black angel sings
And there is no word, no gate anywhere

ECSTASY OF THE PURE

Sleep's huge soft instruments rustle
Through the age-peaked houses
Of men, like snubnosed knives of wool;
And the rock's eyes grind against heaven;
And the water burns;
And the depths are kindled
By what is the spirit of nations
And the wide
Tossing air's eyes that are looking.

Unarmed, the cold priestess weaves
The fish into the pattern of eagles;
And the priestess shines
The eyes of fish. Unfolding here
In heaven O
Touch the face! There is your
Mother.
The golden panther steps with his paws
That are made of silence
Down through the eyes of trees
Into the earth. And this be the sign
Of your death: that you have a love
Less than the naked happenings.

ROGLOLISENDURIKAHRIUM

The pathway. It needs O it needs
Light on it. As a face
We love.

I know the gray panther. He kills,
And it is fun O it is fun
In his heart. As a day
We die through.
Sullen. The deathman is sullen. O
He does not like
Little cars. Cars full of huge snowroses
And men wearing heaven
On their caps.

But joy.

O the joy of roads sweetens the earth
And the panther is a fool
And a fool is that deathman
Who brought us here. For joy
Shall touch every being. As the sun
These fields. O what is a tree and a brook
And a hill and a lamb and a brown sparrow?
What is a pathway?
O look at the beautiful cars O
They are full of strange creatures
Who do not have guns in their hands.

PROGRESS TO A VIEW OF LIFE

Heal the soul, O still-featured host
Whose white desire is to know all being;
O herdsmen of silence and cold light,
Heal the soul of his awful waking . . .
For now I have

A reason to want love;
I have a reason to want peace
And the quiet of the good . . .

There is a tree . . .
A field . . .
The warm hand of this beautiful creature . . .

O there is a hunger . . .
A fiery town . . .
And the hairy fist of this journey
Bloodying the mouth of God

EAT HEARTY

Hey God!
God!

Is that a light?
Can we run there?
Will no one shoot us?
Wait . . .
What sound was that?
Listen . . .
Do you hear it too?
Is it a trick?
Why should anyone call to us?
How can a voice be gentle now?
Not yet . . .
I think the voice is crying.
I think the light is the burning of the world.
I think the voice is your own voice
Crying in the jungles of this human death.

Hey!
Hoooooooooooooooooooooooo

Can you hide us?
Will you promise not to tell them
Where we are?
Can you give us bodies and nations
That no one will want to shoot
Or to drive hot nails through?
Hush . . .
I think the lights of the world are going out,
And the voice of mankind slobbers up from a grave.

DEFINITION OF THE MYSTERY

The words spin the words spin the words spin the words spin the words

Action off the page
Outside the mind

Coming in here
From   where
                                     where?
Train. Bird. Ghost. *Ghost! Flame.* F l a m e
Dry puking soul.
A

Do you have your slippers on?
Suppose the eyes do rot . . .
Reduna reduna gra zunc oeeaooo
All in the mountain mountain
Pretty little creatures PRETTY LITTLE CREATURES
High in the tempest high in the tempest
Pretty little creatures seek God

Dear Night:
am well, and in good spirits.
. . Only something bleeds inside me.
t is getting colder and my hands are as claws tearing at the Face

11

'IN SHADINGS OF AN OBSCURE PUNISHMENT'

In shadings of an obscure punishment
I watch my life choose its own wakening.
It is strange that only now as the world dies
Do I fill with the blood of my special creature.
I have no neighbor, for I come in a wrong time—
And everything is wounded that I would make clean.

Now is the hour of my templement.
I touch the wild humility of another estate.
And I know how the angels walk
In their silvery seasons.
But I taste the sickness of my fellows,
And I begin to drown in all that demeans them.

Therefore I shall forfeit nothing
If I deal with the wondrous lights
That are beginning to sparkle
Somewhere on an unseen continent.

I listen . . .
They are walking,
The jolly ones from another earth . . .
They come nearer.
I can feel their watery breath on my hands.

TRIAL OF THE CHILL GIANT

Mother
Truth
Joy
Faith

God

THE AGE OF PERICLES

O fields of the sun!
O then in flower
The standing man and the image
Of his talk like a white bird
Bathing in the pools of morning.

These are the friends of the sun.
They rest love—
The white bird lying between us.

All in the shoals wonder finds
Its golden fish. I do walk now
In each green and life of love. O
This crude flesh is small
In my world—Clad in levels
As a child asleep, I put robes
Over the sun. For the sun is a womb
And the mother of other worlds
Than this. Something defiles
The white bird lying between us.

Love shall have rest, and the Greek
Decide to build the new Athens.

EGYPT

Cle—
1600 men to a stone. Please mention
the Nile. Croco—But the slow thing
happens in the air.
Tree slender as light.
Did Cae—? I don't remember
that he came.
I remember the sand.
The limping slaves.
The *exact* condition
of their death.
The terrible thing somehow happens
in the air.
Night in that Egypt. God! how cold
the stars must have been.

Tree slender as life,
and as tall
—green then! Where are the leaves
of that time? Why can't I think
these stars are the same stars?
Where do the souls of men have their spaces?

Shall I be obedient in that silver nudity?

LOCKET

As in the green sky
white queens
think of Fate

so in the womb world runs
and comes to naught

But every all man and brute
sings! For love, that red feather
in the hat of heaven, stabs
the naked rib of this dreaming thing
and O then it
flames (the mouth splintering open) . . .

As in the white sky
gray queens
ponder the life of man

and are not watchful, or very mortal at all
to judge of him who only really dies

THE SHAPES AND INTENSITIES OF THIS MAN, THIS CONFUCIUS

However that principle of reason
Which we receive from the sky . . .
That unalterable target,
And in us tranquil
The harmony of result—Who brightens
Your perfection? What produces
The rooted order of the good action?
Is man evil, or the world?
Do I write in my system?
Does any other direct me?
Have I followed my own footsteps
In a land which I do not know?
Should I do the life I seem to have,
Or does it hold holes in my real fabric?

If the truth is inside,
And the form outside,
What is the truth of sleep?

What is the truth in the flame
Which eats at your rejoicing forms?

LAO TSZE

Water!
Star!

and somewhere near now nodding
the moon

The fool
forgets
his man of ice

I weep for the world
O I weep for the world and a yellow spider
makes a web in my heart

I am hurt
I know what is knowledge
·but wisdom fattens the soul of man
O wisdom is the plaything of the fool
The talk
topples
into the water and its ripples fashion
the snouts of monstrous fish

I am indifferent to the death of your world.
Stain!

Clean!

MOHAMMED

And to the kings of the world,
My greeting . . .
The Kaaba shall be thrown into the sea.

These are the dusty little streets of Medina.
Here my people live.
They are poor;
But riches wait in the One True God.
All men are one man in His wisdom.

My wives have soft breasts.
Their hair smells of my sweat.
I place my hands upon their eyes
And they know my hands; what
Is kind in them, what blackened
By my greed and cunning. For
I am a man of thirsts and hungers.

And to the great of the world,
My greeting . . .
The temples of God glow through the night.

INDIA

Over the Khyber
Birds wheel in silken joy . . .
Tribute of another Prince than
Held the Punjab whole—But
A sluggish dark settles over
The plains of Asoka.

A sweaty stain covers the bed
Where the sun had lain.
Horsemen in filthy coats
Do not gleam. The lips of women
Go black under whips. The sun's
Eye goes out. Apparel of hunger
Clothes mankind. O thou (slaying)
Ascend the red air—no star frolics
Anywhere in thy containment.
Both heat and child chill
In thy branches. Sayeth God (*staying*)!
O thus crieth the spirit of murder
In that ancient gentle air.

THE AUTHORITY OF KRAJOVA

That time I made the winter journey
Into his village,
The red breath from my mouth
Stood on the snow like a shaking hand.
The first of his dogs bit through
My coat, tearing the flesh
Out of my wing sockets—and I shot it
Without anger. It was gray with little
Spinning blobs of yellow along the spine.

Krajova was hidden in a tree.
The deer were singing
In mountainous drifts. I knelt in the dark
And told his wife I had crossed the world
To see him. He is looking at something
In the air, she said; he will not know you.

I am not fooled by the singing of the deer,
I told her; it is too cold to be in a tree.
Then I shook the tree—
And a shrivelled little skull fell into the snow.

This is the authority of Krajova! I shouted,
And I laughed bitterly.
But the deer are not singing now, a voice said.

MIRRU

I tip-toed into her sleep
And she was a little girl
Listening to her father clearing the snow
From the sidewalk in front of their house
And it was sweetly mixed-up
With funnypapers on Sunday morning
And black, surly-friendly tomcats
Smelling of New England and
Finnish bread but Finns talk too long
And little girls get tired and father calls
I'll be asleep before you will
And after a moment calls again
Aren't you asleep yet? and when you say no
He adds triumphantly
I told you I'd win, *I'm* asleep
Leaving you to puzzle over it
And later when she has nearly 'grown-up'
Sitting with her mother in the warm kitchen
Reading Mystery Stories and father asking
Are you two going to stay up all night?
And her mother assuring him that
Just as soon as this chapter is finished
We'll stop but somehow they never did
And holding squirmy little flower-eyed rabbits

And watching for Santa Claus at the front door
While the snow swirled so prettily on the lawn
Like a white queen in a beautiful dress

PLEASURES OF THIS GENTLE DAY

I expected to be greeted by one of the figures
Which stood beside the pier; more since
Their formal, black coats seemed to demand
A recognition, than because their presence
Had any interest for me. It was not caution
Which made them quiet; but the strange instance
That they could not speak—for they were stomaches,
And though clothed in fashion, their circumstance
Was not turned from the ordinary pursuits of such;
Indeed, as I bent to inspect the sodden planks
Of the ancient sea-bridge, I felt my hand taken
In soft horrible lips. Then I ran out across
The water. As far as the world is from sleep
I ran. The air breathed. It was not dark
But the light covered my eyes like a wound.
I seemed to look at a procession of maidens
Which issued from tiny caves behind life;
And beautiful lions were on fire at the steps
Of that house where the Great One had His love.
If you do not turn back now, something said,
Another use will be made of your forlornness;
But I had the touch of birds in my mouth,
And a
Heart was beating in my heart.
A languorous turning of arms . . .
Scaffolding . . . the dark music
Unfolds . . . hoofmarks on the black air . . .
Light on the other side of the
Sun . . . the creamy blood of statues . . . far-off,

Classic (neither to thaw nor to be tarnished),
Hard landscape of the *Other Iliad*),
Shadowless breast of the goddess . . . And
The masks are all in place (maturity
Of the carrien . . . companionless agony
In the charnel-houses of this day . . . soggy bread
Upon the matted tables of Ajanta). Yoh!
And walk upon the lea

Father Son flow bleed

Fled

bark fool   bzzzzz

                          and the land of our
tight slowsoft luv   IN THIS WHOLLY GHOST

the stone deer drowse

to hunger

should fall so white a queen
O shudd fall so white a queen

O shudd fall so white a queen

O shudd fall so white a queen

O shudd fall so white a queen

O shudd fall so white a queen

O shudd fall so white a queen

O shudd fall so white a queen

THE DESTRUCTION OF CARTHAGE

Six days out of all the days.
250,000 people butchered in the streets.
The blood reached as high as the chest
Of a tall horse. The women were
Ripped open like fish—after a crude love
Had been performed.

It had an importance, I suppose.
Walls
Around walls.
What was law.
What men did.

Six days out of all the days.
The way a great city dies . . .
Bodies floating through the red churning
Of excited horses.
Perhaps the most horrible thing
Was the excitement of the horses.
That may have an importance
Which will destroy all of us.

THE EMPIRE OF PERSIA

Thermopylae is a well
of agony.
Leonidas is dying;
it is a common death;
he was not a great man.

But there are other matters to consider:
the role played by the rain
—(the wounded, of course—but the wounded
all died—it was an event indeed. Xerses
went on to Athens and this city burned
"to the ground".)
and the part taken by the famous Spartan
idiot
which sat smiling at a blue angel
who unaccountably persisted in drawing
on and off a pair of glass gloves.

Sit then, Darius, on your throne of empire.
The wounded die
and the rain rains; but the smell
of blood does not fade.
It is always the great men who fail.

THE ABANDONED FOREST

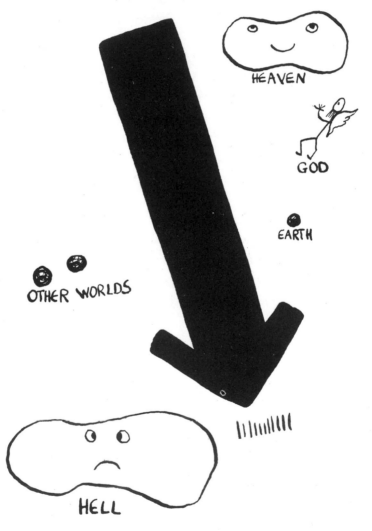

GAUTAMA IN THE DEER PARK AT BENARES

In a hut of mud and fire
Sits this single man—"Not to want
Money, to want a life in the world,
To want no trinkets on my name"—
And he was rich; his life lives where
Death cannot go; his honor stares
At the sun.

The fawn sleeps. The little winds
Ruffle the earth's green hair. It is
Wonderful to live. My sword rusts
In the pleasant rain. I shall not think
Anymore. I touch the face of my friend;
He shows his dirty teeth as he scratches
At a flea—and we grin. It is warm
And the rice stirs usefully in our bellies.

The fawn raises its head—the sun floods
Its soft eye with the kingdoms of life—
I think we should all go to sleep now,
And not care anymore.

ATTILA

The hairy full stern face
Of the Hun.
The wonderful feasts and the singing
Of his bards.
I am the ruthless one,
Butcher of the weak.
I sought life,
And crushed it in my fist.
None stood against me;
I, Attila . . .

Light bubbles up in the east,
And in my tents men harness death
To their scarred arms—Aquileia,
Troyes, Padua—the caverned flames
And the buzzing plunder. It is
Good to feel the juice of thick roasts
On my chin; to shake the bells of power
In the face of the twittering world.

And I died peacefully in the arms
Of a beautiful young woman.

THE APPIAN WAY

The power!
The power alone.
 A road is nothing. A people are nothing.
You will remember that six thousand
Soldiers of Sparta were nailed to posts
And crucified
Along this majestic floor of stone.
But you will not remember the shadows
They made . . . or their cries!
But I think of the road too.
Of the stones.
The legions of Marius, of Sulla,
Lucullus, Crassus—"the Roman
Might" . . . I think of the stones,
Where they came from, who shaped
Their edges. I wonder what man
Stood in the howling of Rome,
And bent down to touch the stones.
He was a man of power.

Who for their living lived
In joy
On a green ground.

O all in the heaven honey
Ate
With angels sweet and merry-heated.

In bluewhite January
They made their whole year.
Snowborn in that small,
Their lives were living.
In their going went God.

Who for their leading led
Pretty animals
Across the playing skies.

O each in that tower talling
Lay
And their kindling made love kind.

Who for their feeling felt
The caress
Of all hidden and happy creaturedom.

THE FIRST CRUSADES

This is the Cross!
The Turkish horde
Holding the Body and the Blood . . .
We the common people moving on the armies
Of darkness and sin—into Hungary
To murder and loot—
And we were butchered by the soldiers.
Now into the Rhineland,
Where we murdered the Jews—
And in turn were killed by the soldiers.
We put Antioch to siege;
Under new leaders, stormed Jerusalem—
And we entered the Church of the Holy Sepulchre,
Stepping over the bodies of the Heathen dead.

The Cross!
A dirty piece of wood
In the hands of a madman . . .
We knew not what we did—
And the soldiers laughed at our screams.

THE CREATION OF AFRICA

When the flame
falls
and it falls O it flies
down
as a blade
laid deep
in the full wound of this dark world

Not at all to say
that I don't stand here
that I don't stab
into the light O in the long wonder drinking
the pretty fire of these creatures
who wait in the light
until they are born
and what is black wilts
as all evil will

You are told no way no law no king
or the will of kings and laws and ways
can keep creation out of Africa

and I make this to kill the cheats among you

ANUBIS

Then dies Osiris
To live. (This again and again.)
Hathor feeds the star
The sea loves. (And light again
And again the light!) There is no end
To life.

A little sound of death . . . Can black Anubis
See death? O my fair, my double-hearted
Dark One . . .
O Queen in Egypt, with the bag of a cow
Between your knees, does death
Fondle you in the sweet woods
Of heaven? (For again and again
Life through death into life.) I turn
Now to an interest in chubby monsters.
I buckle a grave around my neck
And sniff the odor of my rotting.
There is something to laugh at
But the flaming Huntsman has my life
In his teeth. I move my head slyly . . .
But again and again He spits me out.

THE SLUMS

That should be obvious.
Of course it won't.
Any fool knows that.
Even in the winter.
Consider for a moment.
What?
Consider what!
They never have.
Why now?
Certainly it means nothing.
It's all a lie.
What else could it be?
That's right.
Sure.
Any way you look at it.
A silk hat.
A fat belly.
A nice church to squat in.
My holy ass . . .
What should they care about?
It's quaint.
Twelve kids on a fire escape . . .
Flowers on the windowsill . . .
You're damn right.
That's the way it is.
That's just the way it is.

THE MEETING OF THE ROSES AND THE BLIND ANGEL

THE NERVOUSNESSES OF MEMORY

My mother . . . (thy uneasy rust) . . .
I am patient with the angers of the mill
And with the honors of a dirty town
But I am worth something too . . .

I think the jewelry of hunger
Furnishes grace nowhere. Shelter me . . .
These are not false; they are ugly, cruel,
True to every evilness, these, my people,
My blood degree . . . they are what I am,
And what I will not be.

Class in English . . . (the lust of sparrows) . . .
The savage church and the sheriffs
Growing on the red vine of property . . .
A borrowed book . . . all I gathered,
The violet-fingered misery of the child,
The beautiful mystery of girls,
And ever a center in me—
To touch, feel, taste—that would do
What I willed done.

The doors painted with sickness
And unpaid rent . . .
Procuration of my indifferent slave.
But my native I am to cherish a finer realm.

The big lad with too much face
And a voice fuzzed like a slice of grand larceny,
Pointed his fork at the counterjohnny,
Gulped twice, and said,
"Mice think the same as we do."
The countercluck drew one medium light,
Slopped it up nice all over the saucer,
Managed to get his thumb in to the V,
And slide it over to a girl with brown hair
In a cutaway middyblouse tan mesh stockings
Lowheeled suede shoes candystick skirt
And a shoulderstrap purse who had been crying.
Beef went on, "Just because they're small,
And they ain't around much, most people
Most likely hardly know a mouse thinks at all."
Counter turned up the radio and the girl dug down
For her coffeenickel: '. . . of a why-it Chris-mus.'
"You got any ideas about mice?" the face asked her.
"Yeah, I got plentya ideas about both rats and mice."
He started with her rump and his eyes smacked
Their wire-lashed lips: "Maybe you could eat something?"
"Maybe I could . . . in the morning too."
"Sure thing. What you think I am, a piker?"
"Yeah, I know you're a piker."
She ate the hot pork on white with mashed,
Didn't want applepie or danish or cherry jello,
And the mouseboy left no tip when they went out.

THE PRIZE

There are no losses.
There is only life.

Pear-smooth, cool face of a child . . .
Black cow wading in a green pond . . .
The crazy loft in an old building . . .
Sea comin in, honey
O Lord sea comin in
You will find the Lion
O Lord you will find the lion
And war! War?
What is lost now is the world in this time.
Any peace they make is a lie.
Butchers are not interested in freedom;
The higher their talk, the bloodier their aims.
'Why don't you lead me to that rock?'

But there can be no losses.
There is only life for all men!

THE BATTLE OF (   )

Stirred . . . the fur-toothed graves
Of young boys . . . a thousand slain
In the time it would take to do love
With a pretty girl
Or think of a new God. The leagues
Of carrying the slaughter has . . . these fallen
Meanly touch death, their dying
Is such a used thing . . . O the moonplains
Of wandering their terrible hour chooses . . . This
Is a man. You are not to kill him.

This is a man. He has a poor time in the world.
You are not to kill him.
This is a man. There is a purpose in his being here.
You are not to kill him.

Eyes of the wounded . . . the shining tree
Rooted up by a monster. Shall they manage
To lie here in the rain? What do they cross to
In the smoke of so much terror?
This is a m a n. You are not to kill him.

THE BATTLE OF ISSUS

The advantage of the emperor
Eats roses from a red bowl
Which an idiot has to hold the wind in.

Something is rewarded.
The wounded in shining consternation
Mount the black horses of death.
The brave are a little drunk in their chariots . . .
Trained panthers move through the dark commonwealths
Of murder, sloshing the spital of empire on their gray tongues.

Something is made captive.
(The stars howl in their cold towers,
And the naked slain return allegiance
To their Father of Fire—Why didst Thou!
. . . Kiss of the blind leper . . . The face of Thy world
Turned to the senseless wall of conquest.)
The advantage of the living man
Picks skulls in a desolate wood
And the idiot alone has eyes to hold the horror in.

. . . The brave are a little dead in their chariots.

IN

Shove at the flaming thing! That which is highest may alone be fought for. No combat
is worthy in which men of inferior aims engage. To be holy, be wholly your own.
from 'The Assassins' Handbook'

Eternally given. Seek
The flowers of the

Soul.

Be an eye. Say
Soul. It is a fearful thing.
Hard and warm, it takes men
To do.

Moving weary the birds of men
Are too full of war to know
Flying.

These are lain in broken streets
Where death fills his jolly
Hands. He smiles. But love
Weeps.

Life and youth and the souls of men
Weep,
And are not comforted.

'WHEN THE STONES BURST INTO FLAME'

When the stones burst into flame
And the tameless meets his destroyer,
Will light break the star
And will the honor of men
Thunder at doors O will the good
Be dancing and the beautiful a shout
Spinning all their thieving cold thrones

Suck at the blood.
Eat God.
Why sun?

Broken . . .
La. La. Li. Saw a man die.
Bought a tree.

My friend, my mother, my space,
My abundance . . . (What is hurt?
O sing glorious!)
The stones burn in the fire
Of His overwhelming O the grass
Is dancing in the streets of my gray walking.

TO THE GERMAN PEOPLE

Is it tomorrow yet?
Is rain?
Is love?

Hands have lives to warm.
Joy builds a star.
Be well.
Speak of heaven.
The music weeps.

I blow on the hour.
Have sweetness.
It is tomorrow somewhere.
The wound will sleep.

MERCHANT OF ORCHARDS

Birds fly with a better grace in water than in the air; and this needs no demonstration
to the faithful of God.

Denegas Favin

The sweet weariness of the snow
Cloaks the teamsters
Who have just driven down from heaven.
They stop in the blue square of the village
To water their horses. Two of them are wearing
Badges on their caps, which read:
We Poison Flags At Reasonable Rates.
The bride of their chief is naked.
Her hair streams forth over the dogs
Which seem to be troubled by wounds.
In the house where everybody lives
A tame little thing is patting graves
Into shape. "Follow me." We have cared
For life.

I am the other.
The teamsters are mine. Someone is blowing up
These pretty villages. Water horses. Seem to be
Troubled. A naked bride. Badges. Everybody's
House. What is saying
"Follow me."?
Will the snow . . ?
Merchard of ormants
"God break this time of sorrow."

God be a flame

THE MAN WITH THE GOLDEN ADAM'S APPLE

There were four crates of chickens
Hanging from the topmost bough
Of an elm tree near the fairgrounds;
A Mack truck with a badly damaged fender
Was just pulling to a stop across the road,
When a lightly-clad old lady, her shawl
Draped like a tired wing, and with hip-boots
Of bright yellow fur on her shrivelled-up legs,
Suddenly transformed herself into a shepherd boy,
And went crazy-running off over the horizon.
At that precise moment a door opened in the sky,
And the man with the golden adam's apple
Stepped briskly down.

The driver of the Mack backed into a turnoff,
Gunned her up so hard she blew the muffler,
And then slouched limp at the big wheel,
A tiny black hole appearing 'as if by magic'
In the middle of his forehead.
T m w t g a a holstered his deadly automatic,
Swore softly, and taking out a purple bandana,
Removed something from the crown of his Homberg.
He did not even then look up at the chickens;
Instead, being a fellow with a keen sense of proportion,
And mindful ever of his responsibility to society,
He built a fire and set up light-housekeeping in it.

O stars clouds sun dream God

LANDSCAPE

writhing in agony on the red ground

of

the work of the workman trampled to nothingness

the

PERMANENT

It is a man

who is lying here with his face

HERO

shot away

THE SEA

flowers

WINDS

And the beautiful names of women!

48

WHERE TWO O'CLOCK CAME FROM

The seventh dragon turned to his wife,
And, brushing a cloud out of her hair,
Said, If you think that much coal
Will last the winter, then you ought
To have your scales rechecked.
She burst into fire
And her tongue singed the beard
Of a crabby old gelbus who had his home
In a hollow hole. He sighed wearily
And quick-tailed the sky down.
You should not have done that,
The dragon's wife said; it looks pretty
Bare the way it is up there now.
But they could see some creatures
Sitting at a big table in the air,
And they were fumbling around
With something that looked like a clock.
It's a clock! shouted the old gelbus—
(No flies on him)—What time is it, boys?
We haven't decided yet, they yelled happily.
Make it nice and early, said the dragon;
And his wife called up, That suits me, too.
Then two it is, the creatures sang merrily,
Putting their faces inside the clock
And upsetting the table in their eagerness to find it.

THE CASTLES OF DEALEKORI

Under their grim spires, which are bent
By the knavish wind into hands
Inquiring the true hour of God,
A beautiful life . . .
No, rather, a frightening life commands
The attention of Dealekori's people.
For something turns in the heavens
Over that pretty town;
Something is dying up there so very high
Above all accepted enterprises.
Even when Keleeda is hanging clothes
On the great wire that stretches
From the dead's land into the castle garden,
Her white eyes ever seek the upper airs,
And her heart does not feel through light
O every singing wish to wake the stars.
Nor as the arms, the great arms of Jemett,
Close over her tiny breast, does she know
What in the womb of her mother made flowers
O dancing flowers curled to greet the sun.
It is not hard to understand an ordinary circle
Such as the devilmen have traced
On all the threshing-floors of that district,
Because when the harvesters come
In their fat green wagons, it is the pleasure
Of the season to dump the grain in fixed limits;
But when, as so often happens in gentle places,
The skill of the husbander is not adequate
To the unvarying design of his work,

A certain quantity of wheat or barley
Or rye, as the case is, will spill outside
The circle.
Then the agony of the heavenly creature
Rends the most careless heart; and
Keleeda stirs under the driving ribs
Of her beloved like a bird caught in fire;
Yet, Jemett, whose training for manhood
Would startle an angel with its thoroughness,
Does not quickly release her—instead,
His face brutal in the soft dull light,
He . . .
O look! There! The howling Thing
Is beginning to fall! . . .
The graceful halls and sparkling domes
Of the beautiful Dealekori
Are spiredeep in Its blood

'WE FOLLOWED HER TO THE WOOD'

We followed her to the wood
But she dug a hole
And put your father's body in it.

STATECRAFT

The orders of execution
Cannot be carried out
Until the victim consents to officiate.

'DREARY THE HOUR, THE PATH TO SPLENDOR'

Dreary the hour, the path to splendor
Glittering out of reach . . .
Thy footsteps are wrapped in horizons
But snakes piss in mine.

COOL BROWS QUAKE NOT

The stars drive upon the pasturage
Of another shepherd than God is.

'WHAT GIVES THE RIVER RIVER'

What gives the river river   .
And the darkness its dark,
Will have a worldsize life to put my love in.

OPERATION OF THE HUMAN BEING

I was in breath

lying on the face of thy face

I ate the name

I gladdened the naked in mountains

my shoulders overweighed death's
statue in the shrouded weather . . . It is
established as the drowned fashion holes in water
for the eyes of God to look through

'THE STARS ARE OCCUPIED'

The stars are occupied
In their veritable work,
But the great man is not guided.
He may be thrown aside—
And thus leave his creature
In the silent house of art
To weary itself with honor.

FLOURISH IN THY SEASON

Going and returning

tribes of dirt
tribes of shining

death over
all things

but you are made higher
than his wan distance

for you are the height and the distance
where all high things have their doing

'THE ANCIENT WHIM OF MAN'S WILL'

The ancient whim of man's will
To throw death down all his lively roads,
Has placed strange arms on his creature.
Worshippers of the moon, his bloody crying
Has teased new destructions to the earth;
It may appear that what he has life in,
And where he turns, will, like the moon,
Seem to have its life only when it is dead.

Perhaps death is the true condition of man's life . . .

'HOLD THY TONGUE, DEATH!'

Hold thy tongue, death!
Is it clear that you must not touch
The subjects of my dominion—
All her fair soft beauty . . .
The way her eyes look at me . . .

'FOR WHOSE ADORNMENT'

For whose adornment the mouths
Of roses open in languorous speech;
And from whose grace the trees of heaven
Learn their white standing

(I must go now to cash in the milk bottles
So I can phone somebody
For enough money for our supper.)

'OF THE SAME BEAUTY WERE STARS MADE'

Of the same beauty were stars made
That they might guide their earthly sister
When she undertook the white still journey
Into the country of His gentle keeping.

FOR THE GRADUATING CLASS AT HARVARD

It is truly dark.
The scene at the head-year
Did battle to justice.
That should be said—
In honor's interest.
But tell me what you are doing,
With your damn little wizened-up legs
Going at such a pace—
Do you think it matters what cliff you jump off?

'MEASURE THE KINGS'

Measure the kings.
Spill favor on the virtuous.
Root up every obligation but your own.
You are in service to your highest intelligence—
And you will be punished accordingly.

'O YE WILD SKY!'

O ye wild sky!
Breathe, shining animal of the heavens!
Drink of my blood.
O make my life burn in this awful night!

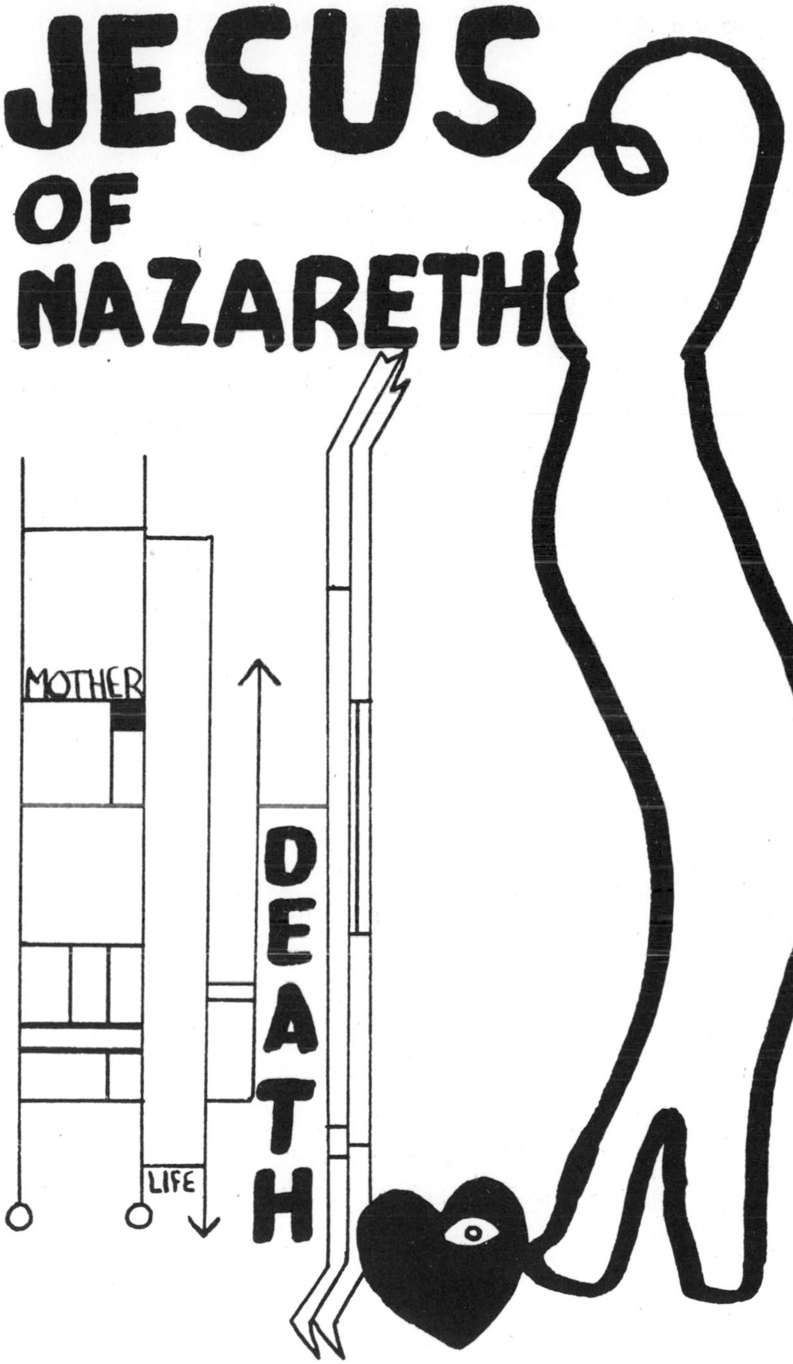
JESUS
OF
NAZARETH
MOTHER
LIFE
DEATH

THE EXISTENCE OF PERFECTION

The forms of ever never
Change.
Long gets shorter, and shorter
Longer. The products of the best
Follow the shape of heaven, making it higher
That they may lessen— to get tall again.

TO A CERTAIN SECTION OF OUR POPULATION

It is ordered now
That you push your beliefs
Up out of the filth high enough
For the inchworm to get their measure.

TO ENLIGHTEN GNASHVILLE, TENNESSEE

The birds lower nets
To snare the wild man in.
But he hits his teeth out
With little fur hammers,
And his heart grows a hand
To shake God's.

'ATTEMPT IT IN FEAR'

Attempt it in fear . . .

Ears . . .
Toes . . .
Scream   when   it
Touches you

'THE MULE OF WATER'

The mule of water
Kicks his blustering heels
Into the snoutsmug faces of His Majesty's
Fleet . . . and their chins, which recede,
Drip a white cold blood onto his scornful flanks.

'THE TASTE OF WOOD'

The taste of wood
Filled the mouths of old cities.
People had houses to touch
Like trees in a gentle forest;
And their hands knew the love of things.
What fills the mouths of our cities?
What can we touch
That will give fashion to any creature?

'O MY DARLING TROUBLES HEAVEN WITH HER LOVELINESS'

O my darling troubles heaven
With her loveliness

She is made of such cloth
That the angels cry to see her

Little gods dwell where she moves
And their hands open golden boxes
For me to lie in

She is built of lilies and candy doves
And the youngest star wakens in her hair

She calls me with the music of silver bells
And at night we step into other worlds
Like birds flying through the red and yellow air
Of childhood

O she touches me with the tips of wonder
And the angels cuddle like sleepy kittens
At our side

'THE SNOW IS DEEP ON THE GROUND'

The snow is deep on the ground.
Always the light falls
Softly down on the hair of my belovèd.

This is a good world.
The war has failed.
God shall not forget us.
Who made the snow waits where love is.

Only a few go mad.
The sky moves in its whiteness
Like the withered hand of an old king.
God shall not forget us.
Who made the sky knows of our love.

The snow is beautiful on the ground.
And always the lights of heaven glow
Softly down on the hair of my belovèd.

She knows it's
raining and my
room is warm

but she is proud
and beautiful
and I have
no money

'SHE IS THE PRETTIEST OF CREATURES'

She is the prettiest of creatures
All like a queen is she

I have made a paper wheel
And I pin it to her dress

We lie together sometimes
And it is as nice as music
When you are half-asleep

And then we want to cry because
We are so clean and warm
And sometimes it is raining
And the little drops scuttle
Like the feet of angels on the roof

I have made this poem tonight
And I pin it in her hair

For she is the prettiest of creatures
O all like a strange queen is she

WONDERFULLY LIFE O WONDERFULLY LIVING HEAR

The stars in their wanton liveries
Wobble at the marriage-board of God,
As I put my arms around her.

I mean to wake the bellman
Of her sweets O of her tumbling moist hair
And I'll have every bell in the world ringing.

The happy flocks of our shepherd whisper
A lullaby to the silvery companies of heaven,
As I place my love inside her.

I move through the room of this wonder
Of this purity O of this garden-running dear grace
And every proud song in the world is singing.

'O TERRIBLE IS THE HIGHEST THING'

O terrible is the highest thing . . .
So be death beautiful to my love.

His nearing wings disturb my sleep . . .
So be moon bright on her lonely way.

The acts of heaven hasten my pretty fair . . .
So be God bountiful to her sweet quality.

O beautiful is the highest thing . . .
So be the angels blinded in her new holiness.

THINKING ROCK

It is not difficult to come here,
Here by the thinking rock.
It is in the way of all firm things,
Things that go into the soul.
For the souls of all firm things
Have a good way to the rock,
And the rock thinks well of them.
Not only men, but the waters, and the forest,
Have souls; morning, the darkness, rain,
Bear cubs, fog, and the wind: have souls;
And these, too, the rock thinks well of.
Beautifully.
And on the rock sits
The pretty Colleen.
About her head so fair and small
The white eyes of the air whirl
In happy solitude.
Glow deep, soul of man . . .
Let me make you climb
Into the weather
Of the beautiful Colleen.
Upon her breast so round and warm
The green heart of the earth stirs
From a winter sleep.

On a day after my death
I came to the thinking rock,
And, kneeling, kissed
The lovely Colleen.
Tell me, dear, I said,

The manner of this death
That I may not offend his bright circumstance.
Then laughed Colleen,
And she laughed as the sea laughs
When its blue legs encounter a new island,
And she said,
O death is only a word in a dull book . . .
Look! Look!
It is beginning to get beautiful again . . .
It is getting beautiful all over again . . .
Look! it dances!
It touches our faces . . .
O the beautiful again . . .
Always
The life of death dances.

May I lie beside you here, Colleen?
Do my hands offend your maidenhood?
Does my voice betray your innocence?
Because I know there is a place like this,
And as much purity,
And love,
And warmth,
And joy,
And I have seen thee, too, Colleen,
And I have known what to say,
And how to be,
And not to dirty with my hands,
Or my voice, or my anger, or my life,
But I have been weak
And I have wronged the beautiful.

Then she stood tall on the thinking rock,
And she said,
There is no purity in you, no faith,
No wisdom;
There is only the noise of these things.
What is pure cares not to be pure,
What has faith seeks not to believe,
What has wisdom needs less to know
Than to reject its knowledge.

On this day while I am alive, Colleen,
And as all around me hate
Divides the nations of the earth,
And murder shines his bloody claws
On every clean and good thing,
I truly believe
That the beautiful will come again . . .
That nothing can stay its coming . . .
O look; it dances!
It touches your faces . . .
Again and again, the beautiful . . .
Always and always
The life of life and death
Dances O
It so wonderfully cleanly dances.

CORONATION OF THE PROUDEST KING

PLAY THAT THING

SPIRIT AND BLADE OF THE HIGHEST TRUTH

Find

lead towards the singing

        child
        wren
        lake
        how does birth last
to get a god born

Who is the mother!

only the rain

        and the blood
        finally at peace
Where it cries

do we ever arrive on earth at all

BUT THE ARMS NEVER DO. NOR WHAT IS SAID. OR BELIEVED IN. OR MADE LOVE TO. OR PUT DOWN YOUR GULLET. OR INTO A GRAVE

The first lion hates the second lion because he can't be first unless he is second too.

from *The Book of the Wingèd Betrayal*

Who lives on both shores!
House formed like a burden . . .
Pleasure is wise
To part the lips of mice;
But already a ghost moves
In your child.
Brief is the way of man,
And his heart darkly strays
Into the hilling night.

That our trail sickens the real communities
Of the forest and the water . . .
To be a stick . . . To tear the light
And to contain a heart! Yes,
There is nothing to empty. Squeeze
The hairy wrists of this final creeping.
Look up! Is that your bonny feast
Death roots in? Wear your faith
O your flashing born
When you step from between the dripping jaws
Of what you live in.

THE IMPATIENT
EXPLORER

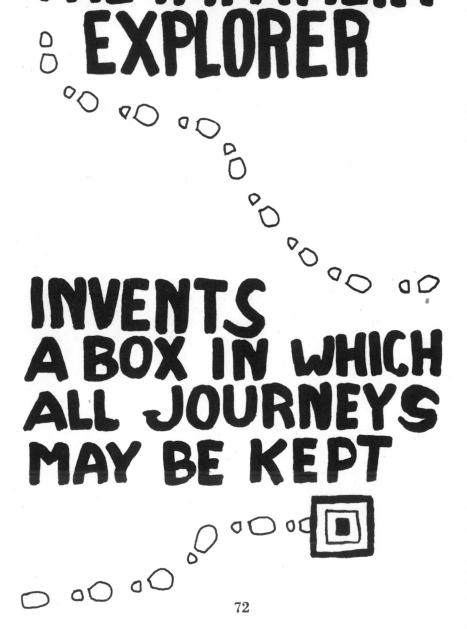

INVENTS
A BOX IN WHICH
ALL JOURNEYS
MAY BE KEPT

I SENT A MENTAL TO MY LOVE

There were majesties.
Rain tilted his shining spears
Into the fat rump of the meadow.
The sheep wooled against one another
In fearful sessions, as
Lightning

Struck
An old tree near the brook
Where we first lay together.
I had not meant to tear her blouse
But she felt so soft and
Pretty, and her mouth tasted
Of blueberries.

The tree was split open like a fish
On a green counter, and in the middle
Of its heart, smiling as on that day,
Her face looked out at me.
Later, and I had cried,
I picked up one of the lambs.
But it only seemed like a thing
One would imagine doing then;
So I put it down as gently as I could,
And started walking fast back to the city.

WHILE THE PANTHER SLEEPS

It is not entirely wrong to think
That there are angels here.
The weather is right for them;
And the panther is asleep.

Walk into the beautiful.
Hold your life out to it.
Put on good like a bird.
Does it amaze you?
Do you really hate God?
O the panther is asleep,
And the soul of man fondles a higher season.

For there are angels around us.
They wear little yellow hats,
And their eyes are made of water.
Give them your doings to hold.
Let them try on your tall.
Will they like to kiss you?
Will your love clothe their fire?
The panther of the world is asleep,
And the spirit hastens to its brightest home.

THE MINSTREL WITH THE CLOVEN HOOF

Thine is the mystery.
O the Beautiful weeps.

Into a ditch . . . mutilated
By thy voice!

Houses swing their wooden lives
Along the black streets . . . fire
     cold
     fogmoons (the breath
     of the mad on our faces)
O lady lady lady
What in my warmth does the wind
Lead? Dowarskillallproudboys . . .
I am naked in a humble grace.
The *deceit*, the *hypocrisy*,—O
I go now
To sing in the house of my father . . .
     (icebirds
     on the white bough
     of death)
     O the war the war the WAR
What in my green realm does reason
Love? I am naked on a hunted ground.

CHOICE OF FORMS

All hidden

Wingèd leopards sing in glittering choirs
              DAY DANCE (now!)

North of heaven
The
Egg
Splinters open

And ——————————— Something sprawls there

FOR UNCLE PRICHARD

The shrines of Hesita
Are torn from their makement cathedrals—
And the pigtree grunts in the orchard of Tedu.
But it is a pretty day in far-off Amerrica.
It is Moonday. The day of the man-blooded fish.
My uncle's nose runs as he motors into Akron
And he blows it pathetically hard into a silk cloth
Which doubles as a windshield-wiper
In case it is a rainy day.
But it is Moonday—day of the goat-voiced feddlepop—
And everybody in Ohio is a little mad. Particularly
My big, wart-nosed uncle. Who is the governor.

76

NOT TO DISTURB THIS GAY GATHERING

O I know a fabulous cowshed
Where a strange beast is kept
That gives milk the color of blood.
And the reason I tell you this
Is that its mate is loose in your world.

'IT IS FULLY PRACTICAL TO CREATE'

It is fully practical to create
That which has form in the silence.
The noise art makes is usually heard
By those whose lives listen to God.
It is not advisable to cheat
That which has no other stake
Than the deeps and brights of all men.

'THE EYES OF CRABS HOLD KINGDOMS'

The eyes of crabs hold kingdoms
Which the highest man cannot see;
Just as the wheels of the moon turn
On a road down which the creatures of heaven
Hurry to their white still gathering.

THE FRIEND OF HEAVEN

In many seasons life moves to the weather
Of Luda
Who cometh forth from life
As dark into the first dark

In many seasons life mounts to the highs
Of Luda
Who moveth forth from life
As death away from death

Alone in all

DEATH AND LUDA AS CONTENDING

Each gift is counted.
The sin quells His white career.
Finger of the Fireland itches
The bone of terror.
Wait.
Run into the fish's womb.
Earth the implements of life.
Heaven death's. He will make you happy.

'THEY DIE. THE LABORS OF GOD'

They die. The labors of God
Shining up through their torn throats
Like a hand fashioning a deer . . .

They die. It is well that man
Put all else away . . .
But war he must not put away,
Because it is wrong to live.

SCRATCH A RICH MAN AND HE'LL BLEED—YOU

. . . . seize the wisest

. . . . flay them!

Secretly.

Tip the heart out.
Set up a machine
To give your wives babies

Then you won't lose a minute
From your labors to get the face of God
Stamped on all your damn currency

UPON BEING TOLD BY A PRETTY GIRL THAT MY POEMS GIVE HER A SINKING FEELING IN THE PIT OF HER STOMACH

The desperate. Of course, the desperate.
It cries a little.
To be real. A stored-up grace. Townly destinies.
Bat carrying a three-day-old angel in its bugged mouth.

O fulliel the gud clear day!
I don't hate anybody.

Yellow light asofting the gloaming
In oldsadsagging Pennsy town.
"God evening, sir."
"Hi, babe."

Don't forget to be happy.
The same always goes on.
That's a pretty light you're wearing.

Let it cry a little, honey . . .

THE UNFULFILLING BRIGHTNESSES

Thy servant I am
Immortal are thy lion-drunk deeps

As a flower thinks
So am I one with thee

Thou art my acquaintance
In the unlevel light

I am falling to sleep
In thy slaying forms

Where goeth the white wind
I have been
And believe

THE BUFFALO THAT WENT TO LIVE AT THE WALDORF ASTORIA

It makes so much noise when I walk
Down the stairs
And the elevator is too damn small altogether.
Maybe I can get them to put in a field
Where the dining room is . . .
A lake would be nice where they have the lobby.
If I asked friends in the way things are now,
They'd laugh at me.
It seems odd that all the trees have been cut down
And there isn't a blade of grass anywhere
Except on the floor of the manager's own room.
My wife complains that the bathtub is so tiny
That there is hardly space for the water to fit,
And none at all for her when the water is in.
Surely the management must realize that to sit
In an empty tub is pretty cold comfort at best,
And the results on the score of personal cleanliness
Are not encouraging from our way of thinking.
It does seem to me that the less I say about the food
The better it will be for the mental climate
Of the maniacs who concoct it:
Tomato sauce on rice pudding! Whipped cream
With devilled lobster! Great mother of the plains
Preserve us!
If my poor father could only taste their crêpes suzettes,
I'm sure he'd demand to be taken off the nickel.
But the watering trough in the Grand Ball Room
Is at once aesthetically satisfying and eminently practical.

IT WAS A BOMBY EVENING

'A fire of birds sweeps down
The haunted wind
And gods of light walk through
This green wood'

Lazy Sam Parmalee

All fine lads in jest upon the yellow world . . .
These bright little cousins of the devil

Storming up like drunken trains
In the high beautiful air . . . and they truly sing
Of one quality for all men O they sing
Of the wide and snarling
Face of death

And we are all turned to their happy accomplice,
To this ordered hate, to this eventfully mortal place

INTENSITY OF THE FOREST

How loving cool in velvet aisles
The flecked pennies of the sun
Sift down onto the coats of green moles

And loose-shrill in the air
The wooden clump of great footsteps
Shakes birds out of God's hand

O now the tiger sings
For O now the tiger sings

Snakes put their cold-soft arms around the fawn
And the high fat laughter of death climbs every hot

O ever sings the tiger of life
And ever louder howls that other, nimbler one

INVESTIGATION OF CERTAIN INTERESTING
QUESTIONS

There were many houses like that in Canlin;
The doors of plated ivory, windows gummed-over
With circus posters dated 1887, fine fountains
Gushing up out of the parlor rooms, chickens
Squatting sunfully on every roof, and the roofs
Shingled on their insides which left the brightly-colored
Wallpaper to amuse the sky and throw merriment
About the hills—but in only one of these houses
Did the lovely Cathy live, and it is to this house
That I lead you now
If you will so honor me . . .
It is a night late in the winter.
Cathy has just hung my coat near the fire,
And I have called hello to her father,
Who is in the pantry fixing himself a snack,
When the phone rings. After a reasonable time,
And nobody answering, it stops ringing.
"Did you have a useful day?" Cathy asks, taking
A book off the shelf and making a hurried comment
In its margin. I open a pack of cigarettes. "Yes and
No. The bargaining didn't get going until nine,
And by then Willowby was in a pretty bad mood,
But I did manage to check up on a few things."
"Do you really think Norden meant what he said?"
"If I knew that I'd have Kain dead to rights
On that Maipoer's affair—but, Cathy, how big
Was the actual turnout? Does it add up anywhere?"
"It adds up to this: if Tynis will make the contact
With Roymer before the fifteenth we shall know
Very definitely what the others hope to get out of it."

"But how can we be sure of Meesy . . . ?"
"Flarr has promised to consult Dykeman and
The odds are Bevens won't even come in on it,
Except to bluff Haggerty into tipping his hand."
"That still leaves Warner and Plinth to furnish
The evidence—it's obvious that Tomkins can't go
To Lannigan without some actual proof that Cark
And Sweet have already told Jalder's brother."
"Cathy!"
"Oh damn, what is it now? Yes, father . . .
Keep your britches on, I'm coming. Excuse me."
"Not at all. He's probably forgotten how to scramble eggs."
She chuckles to herself as she hurries out. Naturally
I fall into the error of my ways and begin a search
For the missing papers—not in the desk; between
The pages of a book? no; nor under the carpet . . .
"What are you doing down on the floor like that?"
"Oh . . . I was just looking for a glass of water."
"Well, you won't find it there; it's over
Under the sofa by the cellarway. And let
The rabbits out as you come past please."
While I stand drinking the water, I kick up
The cover on the rabbit-box. "There're a lot more
Here than you had last time, Cathy," I say,
Trying to keep my feet as they charge by me.
She chuckles to herself again, and this time
I hear her. "What are you snickering about?"
"I'm sorry, but you looked so funny that day
The man was asking you all those questions."
"I don't see what was so funny . . . I did fairly well,
Considering the nerve he had barging in on us."
"You were afraid of him."
"Don't be an idiot, Cathy."

"Then why did you get so angry?"
"Suppose I did . . . who was he to question me?"
"Why were you afraid of him?"
I take three rabbits off the back of my neck,
And drop-kick them into the pantry.
"Cathy!"
"Father, for God's sake! . . . Please excuse me."
"Not at all, I'm sure. Bring me a match, will you?"
"So that's why you've been eating your cigarettes . . ."
Left alone in the room now I stare at the wall.
The snow has drifted in over the body of Cathy's mother,
And the rabbits have fallen asleep in furry bundles.
"Sorry I took so long. Father had another spell."
"I suppose you could have answered his questions?"
"I know what death is."
"It's hardly fair to take the easy ones . . ."
"All right, something hard then."
"The first one he asked me . . . the meaning of life."
"There are as many meanings as there are lives."
"And has each a meaning unto itself?"
"Each life has its meaning in all."
"For Christ's sake, Cathy . . ."
I stroke the cat and toss the bag aside.
"Then you did know Who He was."
I place my arms around her.
"Yes, I knew Him. Please don't cry."
"Nothing seems real or good anymore . . .
Words have meaning, but what is in us
Has no meaning."
I open a marked deck and cut for deal.
"What is in us, Cathy, we know . . .
And words need not know."

ANNA KARENINA AND THE LOVE-SICK RIVER

I bought the river from an old man
For 52¢
Cash money. Housed sensibly in a plow-shed
On my cousin's place, he was happy enough
Until Anna Karenina came to live with us.
It may only have been that the sound and the smell
Of her voice and her hair got under my river's skin;
Or that the way she walked reminded him
Of his pretty home in Minnettha valley;
In any event, in an effort to be realistic
About this thing,
I shall leave the matter of Anna and the river
For a moment to tell you this about myself:
When I was five years old my father got hurt
Very badly in the mill; they carried him in
Through the kitchen of our house—two men
At his head, two at his feet—and carted him upstairs.
The point is this: during the quarter of a century
My father spent in the mills, never once
Did he come from work through the front door;
And the men who brought him home that day
Took the trouble to lug him in by the kitchen.
This is one of the most beautiful things I know about.
Why?
Perhaps because . . .
I'm afraid you've got me there.
Maybe you can tell me why Anna Karenina
Made such a damn dope out of my little river . . ?

AT THE GATES OF THE LUCKY TOWN

all the good books
written in America

a bum
steers

WAKE UP YOUR
LIVER BILE—

fillet of soul

Wilber

worried dog

silly
rabbit
with
shoes

HOW OLD THE WORLD IS! AND BEAUTIFUL EVERY
LASTING THING . . . THE THROAT OF A GIRL; THE
VAST DELICACY OF THE FORESTS; THE PARTS OF
THE EARTH THAT ARE WATER, AND FIELDS, AND
LITTLE TOWNS; THE WAY A MOUTH LOOKS WHEN
YOU BEND TO KISS IT; THE BREATHING OF A
CHILD; THE SILENCE OF THE UNTOUCHED SNOW

A huge head tosses on the roof of the village.
Someone wanders from door to door calling,
Murphy! Murphy! Don't forget the lambchops.
(O we'll all sing one day!)

In a region near the pleasant wall
Two companies of soldiers are getting red.
You know how that goes. But new flutes
For better tunes, eh? Scrub the kitchen, lads,
The house is on fire. (O we'll all sing one day!)

They never get dirty . . . the fancies a man has . . .
Like now I can see a time when all the nations
Of the earth shall live together in peace and love,
And there will be no hatred or murder or fear . . .

A huge head tosses above the roof of the world.
Someone wanders from house to house calling,
    (Etc.)

'THE CARTS OF THE WEE BLIND LASS'

The carts of the wee blind lass
Were covered with silvery wool
That shone on the road
Like sheep walking with God.
Her hair was caught in a fine knot
At the toe of her brain, and her eyes
Had been painted over by imps of heaven.
She held her name in a little dish,
And always at crossings she cried it.

The carts were pulled by horses
Fashioned of mountain-bones
And the anger of yellow eagles.
Their wheels rolled on a single track
That led a little above the air.

And what sell ye, my pretty?
It is nothing I sell, true sir.

Then what do ye bring? lassie say . . .
It is apples I bring. Yet none for you.

Now tell me short the name of this good lad
That I may send him spinning . . .
Then spin the devil, my happy wit;
For my apples are for him.
O take my pretty apples, Mr. Dark!
O all my juicy ripe apples are for thee!

HAVE YOU KILLED YOUR MAN FOR TODAY?

In these hands, the cities; in my weather, the armies
Of better things than die
To the scaly music of war.

The different men, who are dead,
Had cunning; they sought green lives
In a world blacker than your world;
But you have nourished the taste of sickness
Until all other tastes are dull in your mouths;
It is only we who stand outside the steaming tents
Of hypocrisy and murder
Who are 'sick'—
This is the health you want.

Yours is the health of the pig which roots up
The vines that would give him food;
Ours is the sickness of the deer which is shot
Because it is the activity of hunters to shoot him.

In your hands, the cities; in my world, the marching
Of nobler feet than walk down a road
Deep with the corpses of every sane and beautiful thing.

PROMETHEUS REBOUND

It's the feet go to and fro
All up and down the crying weather.

It's the look of the horses
In their white coats eating ice-apples.

Far away and heretofor the bubbling
Brawny grave of everybody's hunting.

O who is the true king in this countrie . . ?

It's the walking of the sweet folk
In their little hidden souls like four turnips.

It's the two who try a green to keep
In the flinging flung winter of their unGodding.

Close at hand and henceforward the anywhering
Weather shall mercy shine until fish walk like men.

Because death is the onlie king in this countrie.

DESCRIPTION
OF THE
HEAVENS

flame

Jump!

TO SAY IF YOU LOVE SOMEONE

O pretty village . . . aye, mine own home . . .
Lamps as yellow as ancient birds . . . here my
Love is . . .
Her breasts grow roses under my hands . . .
Her shoulders have the mark of my teeth upon them . . .
God, jewel the wind to a softer key
That her sleep be ornamented round
As halls the angels splendor in . . .
For we are tired in the green tall play
Of our bodies
And she lies so warm and sweet in my arms

O all the bright summer . . . chamber
Of our kingdom . . . here my maleness
Had its wild design . . . joyful in the land
Of that strangest farmer
A savage wonder made our every climate sing . . .
O God, such is the hospitality of my love
That the husbands of the great mysteries
Built cities near our bed,
And their white chaste daughters spun cloth
That we might be seemly clothed
When we turn from our dazzling occupation

For soon we are going to sleep

NEBISINARENELLITU

House. —————————————— House, and
                                         a dead man in it.

Hill, with
a gallows on it. ————————————— Hill.

Life. ————————————— Life, and no one
                                    to live honestly.

Flame, and
all things dark. ————————————— Flame.

Love. ————————————— Love, and only
                                the murder of men.

The good, and
it is going mad. ————————————— The good.

Youth. ———————————— Youth, and the ground
                             covers its proud singing.

Hope, and what
Shall we hope? ————————————— Hope.

Death. ———————————— Death, and we are
                               commanded to die.

World, and the
lean rifles fondle it. ————————————— World.

Peace. ———————————— Peace, and the soul
                              of man is crying tonight.

Heart, O the time
of sickness is upon us. ————————— Heart.

Man. ———————————— Man, and his works
                             are of no importance now.

Pretty blood O smear
the pretty pretty blood
all over your hands
and into your lives

97

'AH GOD, DEAR BROTHER, THE MILD AND FROWNING ROSE'

In the day of this evil no man a man shall be until his own death is understood to be meaningless to the ends of the State. What is constant for good in him must be denied acquaintance with their undertaking; it is as foolish to die against them as for them. Save when it is in his own conflict—*and for his own purpose.*

from *The Confessions of a Saneman*

Ah, God, dear Brother, the mild and frowning rose
Opens under the golden breath of morning;
Pale clerks and sandy factoryhands rattle turnstiles
In bathtub caves of the I R T; Mrs. Mike Grunnet
Sloshes up the last marble inch in the lobby of R C;
Nasty Ned and Sweet Little Flo pause for a last kiss
Before sheeping out to knock off a lad at 23rd & Nineth
And get those invoices ready for Roberts Produce before ten,
Respectively; armies stir in the hairy thick cancer of Europe,
Their eyes fixed on death, their ears quick to the sound
Of the voice of death; the excellent animal begins the work
Of his day—Ah God, dear brother, the rose that opens here
Is truly the insignia of a terrible garden

What is your share?

Hark ho! Billy Joe . . . why do they chase you?
Funny fox . . . strange tall fox . . .
He died. He died. He really died.

Now you die too.

MAY I ASK YOU A QUESTION, MR. YOUNGS-TOWN SHEET & TUBE?

an grimy houses, shades drawn
ainst the yellow-brown smoke
at blows in
ery minute of every day. And
ery minute of every night. To bake a cake or have a baby,
ith the taste of tar in your mouth. To wash clothes or fix supper,
ith the taste of tar in your mouth. Ah, but the grand funerals . . .
in hitting down
the shiny hearses. "And it's a fine man he was, such a comfort
his old ma.—Struck cold in the flower of his youth." Bedrooms
ay-dim with the rumor of old sweat and urine. Pot roasts
d boiled spuds; *Ranch Romances* and The Bleeding Heart
Our Dear Lord—"Be a good lad . . . run down to Tim's
d get this wee pail filled for your old father now." The kids
me on like the green leaves in the spring, but I'm not spry
ymore and the missus do lose the bloom from her soft cheek.
nd of a Saturday night then, in Tim O'Sullivan's Elite Tavern
            itself:
t is a world of sadness we live in, Micky boy."
ye, that it is. And better we drink to that."
his one more, for home is where I should be now."
ye, but where's the home for the soul of a man!"
t's a frail woman ye act like, my Micky."
nd it be a dumb goose who hasn't a tear to shed this night.")

in dripping down from a rusty evespout
to the gray-fat cinders of the millyard . . .
e dayshift goes on in four minutes.

'THE FURIOUS CROWN CONCEALS ITS THRONE'

The furious crown
Conceals its throne, and I defend
The Dark God.

I take up my arms against
The Christian Three.

This, my offering—*the hairy bull*
Under my knife—the red beautiful flow
Of his blood on the stone altar.
O virgins stirring pitifully in the rude cells
Of my grim faith,
I tell you to prepare yourselves for death.
The hour of my anger is at hand.

I am hunted! O the endless changes
On the shores of my leading . . .
The raging sound of these stained captains . . .
I am beginning to see into the Light!
I am dirty . . . all in murder waits
My rising.
For this is a fire in the houses of your world.

I build a monument for the God of Myself
But Thee I wound

Sink

WHITE

So death (a shining hook) goes
    down crying lanes . . .

His mouth
Bleeds.

Honor him!

He was a  thing.

Touch his heart! thou small fish
Of the American nation . . .

101

THE KNOWLEDGE OF OLD TOWNS

In the eves of the barn
A swallow has her nest.

On the ground sits a little girl.
Her face is buried in her hands
And she weeps bitterly.

An old woman pares her toenails
In the sun.
Her armpits smell of death.

Straight off in the air a valiant army
Moves its thousand sores. Flies stir
On the frenzied banners. Armies
Are not delicious to crack between
Your teeth. The wounded moan
And ask piteously for water.
Words like honor taste like
Hair in their mouths.

The swallow preens her feathers
In the warm sun.

THE IMPUISSANT SURRENDER TO THE NAME AND THE ACT AND THE TENSIONS OF RATHEDA

Hispid ladies in the cold blackened theatre
Pulling on sleeves of fur over their dry
Wrists . . .
Blind watch.
Give a nickel to the sick world.
Give a name to sorrow.

Big is weeping.
Tick tock.

'Twas evening in the meadows.
Rather dull kings chewed their nails
As death got deather and men mener.
Like whipping a spool of snakes.
Or taming a lute.

The show will
At once now without delay begin.
Hoot at the ladies!
Their lives are on backwards.
Like splintered dolls. Like (sweet little po-ets
In the *Southern Non-Partisan Non-Poetry Non-Nothing ReVIEW*).

And in particular ask me to tell you
What I think of the present state of Our American Letters
As I think
It stink—
Together with the drippy jerks who commit it.

RAGAMUFFIN PLAYING WITH A REALLY PRETTY CREATURE

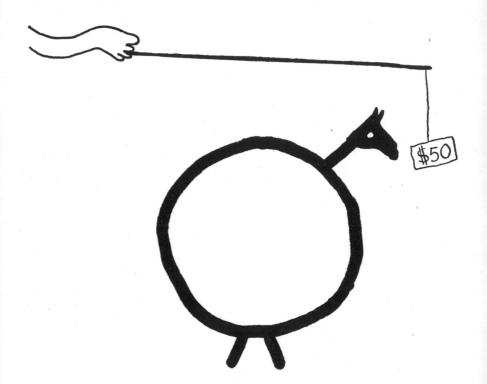

WHILE HIS POOR MOTHER ROAMS THROUGH THE CITY LOOKING FOR WORK

THE CULTURE OF THE MISSLAID PEOPLE

The noise of the grass
Does not disturb
The dead.

"A thing said like that
Can worry the stone goose
Who sits at the door of the world,"
—This from their wise men!

I thought such foolishness
Had had its dome hammered.
You see, it is their custom—and
I speak with authority now—when
A child is three, and just at its softest
Time, they paint its eyes gold and
Sell it to the Evil One.
Yet they get upset when I point out
That the dead are not disturbed
By the noise of the grass.

What the hell do I care
Whether the stone goose is worried or not!

THE TEMPLE OF DIANA

O an untemptable sentry
Walks around the balconies of heaven
And a lean vague dog roots in the dirt
Of the poor . . .

To commemorate thy beauty, O lady
Of a lost city, of a world now dead . . .
Since it is little I do with judgment,
May I claim you pure and of a sin
Such as the angles have: for I am tired
Of these changes—so like stirrings of the dead;
And of the rich—whose greed places Christ
In the skull of the war; for I am tired
Of the poor—who own a world
And have eyes only for the boots of their betrayers.

I am tired of the lies . . . of the dirt
And the murder

I am too angry to bother with this poem
About the beauty of the world
Who cares a damn about that now

NOW I WENT DOWN TO THE RINGSIDE
AND LITTLE HENRY ARMSTRONG WAS THERE

They've got some pretty horses up in the long dark mountains.
Get him, boy!

They've got some nifty riders away yonder on that big sad road.
Get him, boy!

They've got some tall talk off in that damn fine garden.
Get him, boy!

When you can't use your left, then let the right go.
When your arms get tired, hit him with a wing.
When you can't see very good, smell where he is.

They've got some juicy steaks in that nice sweet by-and-by.
Get him, boy!

They've got a lot of poor black lads in that crummy old jailhouse.
Get him, boy!

O they've got a lot of clean bunks up in their big wide blue sky.
That's his number, boy!

LAST YEARS OF THE POET KHIALI

The messengers of Rehu
Hurry their white-footed horses
Down the little mountain roads
Which lead to the rivers of my other life.

The conditions of summer
Are maintained in the Sanaven brothels
Where my youth was spent.
O all golden . . . . ;
. . . . ho! . . . . the pretty breasts
And . . . . ;
. . . . I miss it now! Opposite
The man, always so warm and soft . . .
When the fire of . . . . and their arms . . .
Over the fence with your other pleasures!

I had little real interest in drinking
After the third bottle.
My tame lizard, Teki;
My ball of colored string; my books,
Bound in goat skin, that nobody
Ever bothered to read.

The messengers of Rehu
Will come in their wise time,
And I am content to go where they take me.

CARNIVAL
LATE AT NIGHT

The Bells with silver Sounds the Region shake

See the Bearded Lady

o watch the little towns getting

Sleepy

Is this the right change, God?

yellow RED green dog bear wolf

sweet light

MY COAT IS DIRTY

They had taken off their sandals,
And their naked feet dipped into the black water
Which ran along the earth's other coast.
Those sandals were of angel's skins,
And on the toe of each flamed an infant star.

Two miles away a tree was just beginning to grow,
And I wanted to care in its life
Until the tiger had eaten the sky;
But they said, fingering those sandals so bonny,
You may not leave our side O you may not go
Before man has touched his sparkling career.
That tiger had a crimson voice,
And all the hills about swayed in his talk.

A thousand years away a being had its home,
And I wanted to take it my heart
Because something dwelt there like love
O like when you cry you cry to God alone;
But they told me, wiggling their feet in joy,
You may not know the beautiful
Until you have drowned in the waters of our coast.
Those waters were choked with the skeletons
Of what I thought must be the soul's own creature.

A billion lives away the instruments of perfection
Were readied for the highest human-thing,
And I wanted to kneel down in their light;
But they said, and they tore at my clothes,

You may not think of them O you may not tarnish
Their pure design with your tiny occupation
Until the tiger and the sky and the black water
Have fashioned you a coat that will fit your God.
That coat, which they had torn from my nakedness,
I throw out over the world . . .
And I think it will fit the world.

SPECULATION ON A RAINY DAY

Hidden in the fiery thickets of heaven,
Their gentle mouths covered with bloody fur,
The things of God watch the earth.
Along those high lanes light
Breaks, as in a conflict of monsters
What is in shadow fills with fire.

What do words mean in that awesome space?
What does 'city' mean?
What does 'God' mean?
Or 'life', or 'love', or 'light'?
What does 'man' mean?
What does 'good' mean?
Or 'war', or 'darkness', or 'evil'?

Aglow in the terrible forests of heaven,
Their beautiful eyes filmed over with death,
The things of God watch everyman.
Since all that was good we have defiled,
It may seem that the human house is a cage
In which are chained the monsters of our true animal.

CHATTER

The skin of winter
Is covered with a fine white hair
Which gets into the throat of God—
And He coughs it up over the world.

'NO HONOR MAY BE HAD'

No honor may be had
Except the Highest see it
And mix it well in the dirt between his toes.

THANKSGIVING

The death of gardens
Swells the autumn's rustling pockets—
And the North Wind bends down to kiss
His worm-tainted quarry.

'AND BY FINDING THIS ONE EARTH'

And by finding this one earth
A beautiful board to smear my juice on,
I can only want a broader target
To throw my death at.

HOW TO BE AN ARMY

MANY SHOES   POTATOES   FLAGS & FLEAS

RIFLES   TRENCHES   DETERMINATION

KNOWLEDGE OF MARCHING

$$\$\frac{58207}{27850} = BLOOD$$

+ (GENERALS)

AND A FAITH IN THE RIGHT

115

"AND WHEN FREEDOM IS ACHIEVED . . ."

You have used a word
Which means nothing.
You have given a word
The power to send men to death.
Men are not free who are sent to die.
Only those who send them are 'free'.
You should have freedom stuffed down your fat throats.

AN AVERAGE ENTERTAINMENT

The crawling

Sniff

Is she going to die in that dress?
No. She will remove the dress, place it
On a chair near the window. The window
Will be silently lifted . . .
A hand will   caress her.

'THE ANIMAL I WANTED'

The animal I wanted
Couldn't get into the world . . .
I can hear it crying
When I sit like this away from life.

116

NAINDA

It has in meaning
The moaning of God.

From the sun
Rumors come . . .

Kneel down O kneel
Where the sin is . . .
Sink under where His chill flames

'FILL THE MOUNTAIN'

Fill the mountain
With the names of life.
Grow close to trees.
Birds drink water.
Man has his season.
O fill the mountain
With the names of life.

NOVEMBER IN OHIO

There were twelve ragged children
In the house.
The sleigh tinkled snowily down the street
And they all looked out of the window at it.

CHILDHOOD

In this trouble . . .

Is mother afraid of the lion?
Is it seven o'clock yet?

Does anyone else see him
Padding into her room
On his golden soft feet?

Father gets home from work
At seven . . .
Please tell me what time it is now.

'CLOUD DRONE BOOT RATTLE'

Cloud drone boot rattle
Grab

Watch call fist throttle
Lunge

O plink your little rifle
Killed him
Ah

THIS POOR LIFE; THE RAIN
AND THE SHINING GUIDE:
THE NEST OF THE HORSE AND THE SCALES
OF ETERNITY
MAKE A PATTERN BUT I'VE GOT MY LIFE CAUGHT
IN A ROAD GOING NOWHERE

The empire is
Officially a goddamn bore.

Money's antennae
Feel over the asses of everybody.

As far as that goes a fire ten miles high
Wouldn't warm some of these toads.
They shake my hand and their gloves stink
With the sweat of my people.

They ride a blind horse in a race to hell.
But they sing pretty fat now.
Try tickling me under the chin!
"I just met the most amusing writer . . ."
How perfectly snotty.

For the pittie o' 'em,
O for the pittie of their bloody ways . . .

As now I've said their death—
I'm sure they will know whose friend I am.

THE POON-RIL POEM

I traveled in morning upon the golden robes
Of my wantoning. No other was master
On that loveful ground. Light wearied
In the touching of my swords—O light itself
Was overshone.

Say to the beautiful sunmen of the earth
That an answer flashes above the warring.
Say that I hold my waking armies here
On highroads where a jubilant tiger
Raises his heavenfaring deerdom.

And all the kings of sorrowing
Speed to my China.
I am the neighbor of death's awful cause,
Brother to the wounded,
Father of the damned . . . I am the spider
Whose web swings reason out of the world.

Waiting in the shadow . . .
Preparing a song for the fiery wolf
That watches out of the blackened cave
Of my life.

And it is bitterly . . .
>   for the in-Justice of the lawful
>   lives . . . *to speak openly of God,*
>   *to hate deceit and the treachery*
>   *of those "in high places"—*
Whose 'high'? Whither these gray mice?
These frock-coated numbwits . . .

God
Look at Your proudest animal! Can I
Think of a bird, then a wren—of a wolf,
Then a white one—O a wren a wren
A pretty wren and a wolf a fine wolf
With a black warm heart . . .
For I am truly sick of my own kind.

But I begin to want so much beauty
And love—O how these clustering wings
Lead us to a clean dominion!—I am
Not bitter to be here.

Purity is the occupation of my art.

AFTER A RONDEL BY TIMBERLAKE

What's that that runs
Around the world!
O look! And give to God.

Curling lads and maidens
Lie in the sweet grass.
They love! O give to God.

He who knows the lovèd Lord
Shall claim an honorable grace,
And to the Light show an everlasting convoy.
O live! And give to God.

O the lads have their faces
Blown to bloody tatters.
O look what someone has given God!

LOVES OF THE TRAGIC OWL

Sudgway gray as an angel's leaving—
Sornhom in lake—

Flurddddd—teeth in a slate apple—

Zeeeeen—Stilgrind twing flick. Bleeoook—
Rattlesoft mouth—
Lusssssssssssss lornhen—

Tubititititititit (bloody grass) ferngrim
As an old man's brain—
Sedghart ice-clothed in gray fur—

Soprim bitch—in a perfeast mating—

Send me, coldgraygal—eeeeccccccuuuooo!

2. A great bell beginning to

1. Smoke rising over the quiet hills... RING

away

↓

is death

down

l o w under the water...

EVIL

THE UGLY MUG

a RED BIRD

with a golden throat flying back

fragrant woods

heart of the

off in the

3. and somewhere

and

north above

a poem named HELP YOURSELF TO SUMMER

O TAKE As Much As You Can

124

FOR THE MOTHER OF MY MOTHER'S MOTHER

Wind. Flower. Pretty village.
1847.

This is the autumn, Jenny.
Leaves scratch
The lowest star.
Green are the leaves, Jenny.

Pleasure in a warm young body . . .

Dogs snap
At the sullen moon.
Cruel are the dogs, Jenny.
They do their crazysad love
Over your sleeping face.

Snow. Rain. A bad world.
Jenny, my darling Jenny . . .
Black are the leaves that fall
On your grave.

'THESE ARE MY GREAT ONES'

These are my great ones . . .
days like cabbages rolling out
on the green floor of the world
to be eaten with sunny spoons
in this huge weather
that my joy needs
where I am
its son as a thin cord
the kite's
and a god on a pale fence
watching
death and life romp through the bright pasturage of towns
and seas and flakes of boys teasing a giant who holds a bloody gun
to the head of my hunting O look I have found
a pretty creature I think it is a man though the face
has been shot away and the hands are not caressing anything
beautiful they are caressing
a grave and the light does not come here O now you will need them
my great ones and I say take them take them put your tongue
on their fulness O there is a beautiful
and it lives in simple things
an orchard of sweet pears
a hut on the fragrant shore of the woods
girls with straw bonnets picking Queen-Ann's-Lace
and the lives of men
and the lives of this year and of the next thousand years O
and the lives and the deaths of all things on earth

'AND THE ANGEL SAID'

And the angel said,
Gnritotavuleylanmwizse,
Whuk b-soun mhi tilnpvobiiad;
O ralh ofykizooceumhedll.
Somg yothbea stakonlrn; lif: Cr . . .
But we did not accept
The star.

We did not accept the star at all,
Because we were not going home.
We did not accept the star,
Because we had no homes in the world.
S i l e n t l y
P u t t i n g   :
O u r   h a n d s
O n the beautiful face
O   f
T   h e
.A   n   g   e   l.

Because we had no homes in the world,
We could not accept the star.

Because we were never going home at all.

The mame! Club

Brother

to live...

Evening Star

i from a

Beach

MORNING

Grain

O should fall so beautiful

Metal

INDIA

Flower The fire! O the fire!

AVE MARIA

128

THE FAMOUS WEMEZETTA ZOO

My grandmother walked down the brass steps
That led past the headkeeper's shanty.
Her lace waist shone like a snow fire;
And her neat red lips
Were ever so slightly open.
She had been dead for almost an hour.
The bindy bear reared on his legs,
And a pilder pooed him. Two serpents
Were making babies near the pop
Corn stand; however, as it got dark,
The wolfgirl growled once, and a deer
Went to sleep
As the

Voice spoke;
And it said,
All things must die.
Death takes all things.
My grandmother smiled almost shyly,
And she put her hand on the greatest tiger;
Nothing dies that is beautiful, she said.
Then the voice laughed,
And it said, what is beautiful but death?
His life, my grandmother answered,
And where it is he cannot go,
Since the life of death is not death at all.

THE MURDER OF TWO MEN BY A YOUNG KID
WEARING LEMON-COLORED GLOVES

Wait.

        Wait.

                    Wait.

   Wait.

    Wait.

                      Wait. Wait.

             Wait.

                    Wait. Wait. Wait. W

           Wait.

      Wait.

           Now.

WORK FOR MOUNTAINS

In One, as One, to One . . . death
And life and the earth in the one One
Whose life is all things having breath
And having death . . .
I am weak in life.
False to my company.
Smell of the animal rots my will.
Thou bind the knives to thy wound
But I praise Thee from many sicknesses
O I praise Thee with the mouths of my name
For the knives in my wound make all my fools chatter

WHEN THE BEAUTIFUL WAKES

Welcome, Luda . . .
Dark of every being . . .
Least of the skying tribes . . .
Savior of no single creature . . .
Born in each hour . . .
In death always . . .
Outside God, God . . .
Faceless on every face . . .
Joyous in thy severing wholeness . . .

'IN HORROR THE GOD-THROWN LIE'

In horror the God-thrown lie
Near the mouth . . .
Its teeth gleam.
In horror the God-thrown lie
Near the white mouth . . .
Its teeth close on their lives.
Its teeth close on their watching lives.

THE CARRIAGE

Foddle-dee the
Dust.
Old man with a flute.
Girl with a silk dress on.
I thought we'd come to a town soon,
But this doesn't seem to be the world
We're driving through now.

'AT THE CAVE'

At the cave
Two weeping things entwine
In gestures of love.
Their eyes are cold as thrones
And blood drips from their wings.

O THAT JESUS-BOY—WHAT A GRIM LAD
TO DROP DOWN INTO A PUDDLE OF SNAKY NITWITS

No creature of lies and compromise!

the uttermost name . . .
in terrible limits . . .
lived (to kill all wars)
lived (to free every man)
near the revengeful Form
endureth as a savage fire
and He endureth for an ever
and He endureth as the maker of revolutions
and He endureth as the God of God in all men

'IN THY FALLING HAVE FLAME'

In thy falling have flame
May thy will O may the pieces grow
On a body again and may thy will rise
In the cold to be a cry and may light
The light of summits
Seize the twins of my naked spirit
To heal O to heal what waketh
Outside the animal

'SEASONING FOR ADVENTURE'

Seasoning for adventure
Is a pack of hounds
Worrying a little blind girl
At the edge of quicksand;
Or memorizing The Four Freedoms
In Hindustani.

'THE HOME OF MY SPIRIT'

The home of my spirit
Is not on the earth.
The home of my spirit
Is on the earth of another time
And world.
When it is home
I shall have none.

WHO SEES THE FOOL SEES THROUGH THE FIRE

The wild air
Fills with my journeying.
My king looks at his country,
And the cold lights of heaven
Blaze down on his serene face.

WHEN WILL THE WATER COME IN?

Serpent . . . heart and face
of the serpent-power

in an endless heart and face
above thy city

Son of Love
is dead

I beat at doors. It seems
that everyone is dead

When will the water come in
over so many dead?

SUSTAINER OF CLAY BLESSINGS

Certainly the mother

Opener

In morning flowing
For every angelbeast thing . . . fearing
As all fear

With many lives lighted,
The Luda, the mother

DECISION OF THE BEAUTIFUL

I loot the merciful of his mercy,
The just of his justice,
The lover of his love—
I am settled in the punishment
And I cry against the cry
And I wound the wound I heal

'ENJOYMENT OF WOMEN'

Enjoyment of women
Makes good rooms for life to live in.
Sharp food and pleasant drink
Do town the spirit with clean inhabitants.
For the gloomy man, gloom;
For the kittenish of appetite, soft cozy pretties
To write poems about or to smack around;
People can get springheads in the winter,
And winterheads in the spring;
It all depends on what they have to live with;
But the people who don't like to be people,
Will get messed up in some way or other.

'BRING THE WOMB ITS MOTHER'

Bring the womb its mother.
Raise the sea's child.
A festivity in the beginning town . . .
A conduct for the beautiful generations . . .
Not like fog.
Not like weapons in the hands of a fish.
But like weapons in the hands of a star.

'IS IT NOT DARLING DEATH'

Is it not darling death
The sons of men gather unto their violent wills?
Is it not his bright belly
They fill with their possessions of rot and tears?

'THE FLOWERS ARE BORN IN SHINING WOMBS'

The flowers are born in shining wombs . . .
O what remains to adorn our daughters?

The creations of the lark nourish heaven . . .
O what shall we bring to that fiery landing?

The maidens of death wear birds on their mouths . . .
O what shall we taste in that cold white kissing?

'WHAT NAME, LIGHT?'

What name, Light?
Murder flees murder—divided in thrones

Stirs the master. Question him!
Aim in the kiss a child gives summer—murder
Yellows the soul of man.

Where is your father, Light?
Like any other disaster we watch the claws
Come near

THE LIVELY ENCHANTERS

As an example of delight, the selection
Of plump maidens to be cooked
On silver stoves . . . thenas their flesh
Will afford toothsome entertainment
For the more subtle appetite of our leaders.

'HE FEEDS ON ALL'

He feeds on all
Who is himself not fed.
No man surely
Can rescue his own victim.

138

O FILL YOUR SACK WITH TIGER CUBS

Of keeping; the competition of brutal law;
Splendid romp of winter; and the moon—
That cold cat in her twinkling prison,
Eating the slime of women and rubbing
Her creamy fur against the purpose of the world;
When men sleep, and the finer flames—caves,
Too, sad chill brown hair flecking their mouths;
And the rocks, again brown and blown, that are
Like fruit a monster would eat; music
The sea has, the velvet voices of the drowned;
Corks of importance, those ships of Caesar;
Midnight snack of sweet resolve; though I make
No complaint; for there is the cypress and the shadow
Of The Just on the earth; and, curling like
The angry fingers of the whirlpool, the harvest
Of blood awaits the terrible farmers of Their war;
So a faint breathing in the wound; the bannered
Valleys rise to the wind; death fills his clapping lungs
And something cries—O angel deep in the water!

And the snake swings his ghost
Through the loud weather of my running.
I touch the wing.
Now churning tents abide Your reverence.
A little dog, tired of heaven,
Trots into the jewelled head and falls asleep.
Wink wide. Who are these? Why is this
Stolen? My question to You is:
What have You really provided? Just this rag
We wipe our living on . . .

The deribude grass
And the white blind road
Going nowhere. My weapons, my sport, my limits . . .
I intend that You listen!
The leprous eye blooks open . . . (For beauty?
For what is pure?) And it is easier to burn.
Wind blowing through the gray sun . . .
By the flaming rock stands Your terrible child.
Ah wee dear rain wilt thou fall
And falling
Rise again

Above the whale road toss the shabby cathedrals
Of this tempest . . . pulleys—food, love, water,
The greenwhitelonelybrightwindows of the soul . . .
Morning keeps great kiddish flocks
In crazy pens; a fire of birds sweeps down
These haunted lands . . . And it is wiser to burn.

Ferns of hell . . .
The destiny of greasy lads . . . Ropes! Straw! To grin!
It cannot see out
The monsterkind glands of murder spewing into Your sons
As this manscape sickens unto the dark bitch.
Ah wee pure rain wilt thou fall
And falling
Rise ever again

And into the black Fire speak my name

'THE DOGS OF THE SKY'

The dogs of the sky
Run to His will.
They are clumsy
With love of Him.

Their eyes glow above the world.
I turn my heart in knowledge
Of their ways. They watch me.

He tells them to watch me.
They watch me at His command.

They dig in the rubbish of my city.
It seems that what they dig
Is a grave.

THE ENCHANTED MEADOW

HELL

TREE

4 angels on the square

BOY

LAKE

NEW YORK

HEAVEN

142

VITA TRIUMPHATRIX

O all still in the brown meadow . . . the twitching of red deer
on a smoking horizon.
Pails of cold gray fish
raining down
on the villages of the world

Here with my sweetheart!
O here with my sweetheart!
I AM BREAKING OPEN WITH MY JOY IN LIFE!

O I slapped the butt of an angel, an angel . . .
By Christ
Just to fill your lungs with air!

O come on, sing!
Sing you damn hills and trees and stars and piddypots!
Fill your hands with me, O sky and earth and little bitter apples!
I'll chew you to pieces!
O all good and sweet and clean and full of juice and gravy . . .

There isn't enough of things.
There should be more kinds of rabbits and snails and ways
Of walking down a road and touching a girl and knocking
A ball over a fence and eating a plate of spaghetti . . .
O I should have a thousand hands and heads and bellies
For all I want to do and know and be and for all the people
I want to knock the hell down
Or put my arms around

'BE MUSIC, NIGHT'

Be music, night,
That her sleep may go
Where angels have their pale tall choirs

Be a hand, sea,
That her dreams may watch
Thy guidesman touching the green flesh of the world

Be a voice, sky,
That her beauties may be counted
And the stars will tilt their quiet faces
Into the mirror of her loveliness

Be a road, earth,
That her walking may take thee
Where the towns of heaven lift their breathing spires

O be a world and a throne, God,
That her living may find its weather
And the souls of ancient bells in a child's book
Shall lead her into Thy wondrous house

EASY RIDER

They told me I might hold the fairest one
Until the murder got finished down in the valley.
'Down in the valley, valley so low . . .'
But it grew dark that quickly I couldn't see.
To hold anything very well, and the knocking
At the door came on hard through the screams
Of those outside. "Are you afraid, little one?"
I asked her, moving my hand up over the face.
"Not if there be a God," she answered, beginning
To stir in my arms like a cat settling himself.
A blue light went on,
And as quickly off again . . . "Did you see them, too,
My little one?" I whispered. She started to cry
And I took my hand away from the face.
"They were all . . ."
"Yes, little one?"
She didn't speak again and my hand moved up
Over the face. "If there be a God . . ." I said
Very softly into her hair.
Then the door opened and seven came in.
They were usual enough save for their heads
Which glowed like great lamps.
We shook hands in a little circle
And I questioned them about their world.
They smiled almost shyly at me,
Pointing to a spot on the floor.
The tiniest lion I had ever seen
Was sleeping there, its paws closed over
A little ball. "Pick it up," they told me.

I placed her on a thagen chair, smoothing
Out her dress that she might be prim.
"Are you afraid to pick it up?" they said,
And I noticed that their arms had been cut off
At the shoulder. A singing began
As I grabbed the ball away from the tiny lion—
'O away from that tiny lion . . .'
And I felt my life beat in my hand.
'O beat in his fine hand . . .'
I threw it then at the first of seven,
And my mother's face shone at the window;
It seemed to be trying to warn me of something,
But when I ran there it had gone;
And I threw the ball at the second of seven.
My father's body fell out of a cupboard,
And when I ran to help it up, a band
Started to play and soldiers marched
Over it in a very dragon of glee.
The third I threw and my brother said
You're making a fool of yourself when
All this time you could have had a good job . . .
With the fourth and fifth the years I hated
Sprang into my throat and everyone
I had ever betrayed seemed to be crying
All at once — and the sixth I threw —
'And the sixth he threw . . .'
And the seventh—
'*And* the fatal seventh . . .'
Then every dark thing howled and the seven
Put their hands upon her—
"What have you got to eat here anyway?"
They demanded. I gave them warmed-over

Duck and thick slices of thagen bread,
Which they washed down with hard cider.
Soon they were nodding their golden heads
By the fire, and very quietly, not to wake them,
I cranked the phonograph
And put Ma Rainey on.
'O he put Mother Rainey on . . .'
Then I knelt beside my sleeping fair,
And whispered into her hair, "O my little one,
O my pretty one . . ."
But she did not wake,
And my hand moved up again over His face.

LIVES OF THE SWAN
(A Little Song For Myself)

Black teeth
Seek the pale ropes which bind life
To a usual career

I am tired cries the swan
I am tired cries the brutal swan
O I am tired cries the terrible one

I am tired of this white deceit
I am tired of all my silken kind
I am tired of what lives and what dies

What can I do now cries the swan
What can I do now cries the gentle swan
O what can I do now cries that poor lost fool

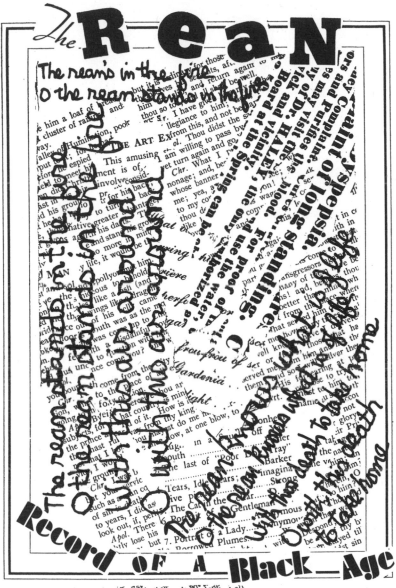

The RΣaN

The rean's in the fire

O the rean stands in the fire

The rean stands in the fire

O the rean stands in the fire

The rean knows about the fire

O the rean knows about the fire

Record of a Black Age

The rean stands in the fire

O the rean stands in the fire

THE SHAPE OF ONE ENTERPRISE

How many breathings
Until the breath stuns the word?
Until the breath stems the wound?
How many dealings
Until the very life is dealt?
Until the vainest love finds a doer?

Little kind of dying . . . .
What a head is.

A little disaster to the stone,
When what you are goes on alone

To stay where all thinking is of the stone

THE COLONY OF THE SUN

We did at last manage to get the eyes
Of Dolina on us, but, as I wrote to my brother,
The misunderstanding was of too old date
To employ his complete sufferance in our cause,
Particularly since Polly and I both grew up
In the Colony of the Sun, and our employment of talk
Had a turn away from the so-called professional world
Into rather better channels, that is, we liked
Each other enough not to want to kill anybody else,
Or to do much of anything except hold our citizenship
In the universe of all men, where the exciting events
Are things like the taste of good food, and the color
Of a girl's hair, and the way cats walk, and forests
Look in rain and snow, and the bearing of the sky
As it fills with stars, and how the earth smells
When you plant something in it—but I'm wandering away
From my story—the very fact that Polly and I
Loved each other was enough to prejudice Dolina
Against us, for he liked neither her nor me; and
That's what this is about.
I first met Polly in a freight elevator in Toledo.
What she was doing in a freight elevator I don't know;
As for me, I had a job running it.
We had dinner that night in Anthony's Chop House
On Lemer Street, near where the old Strand Theatre
Used to be; and it couldn't have been loveatfirstsight
Because I didn't see her again for almost ten years.
A lot of things happened to me in the meantime, of course;
And in a minute I'll tell you what happened to Polly.

151

With me the little wheels went round . . .
I worked in Seattle for a while repairing refrigerators;
In Ft. Worth it was selling ladies' sheer undergarments;
In Richmond, nursemaid to an old gent with a soft pate;
In Tulsa, three months in a Chinese barbershop, shining;
I dove for pearls in a ketchup joint in Saint Louis;
Lumbered a bit up near Thief River Falls;
Then on to Montgomery, Carson City, Pittsburgh,
Memphis, Flagstaff; with shovel, wrench, hammer, drill;
Loaded down with samples of hairtonic, saddlesoap, books,
Filingcabinets, phonographs, jockey's shirts, boots, mouth-
Wash and babypreventers; and it all wasn't smooth
Sailing either—four months in hospitals, two years
In jails, and seven weeks as the husband of a circusfreak
With the oiliest tongue and dimmest brain of any creature
This side of Congress. But I had a better time than Polly.
To put it cold, Polly had gotten round to being a whore
When I saw her again in Colorado. Her face
Had started to fall in, and her eyes looked like stones
Yellowed by the rain. But her teeth were still pretty
Good, and her breath sweetened up when she had been
Away from the bottle for a week. Now, the size
Of a person is what's in him, and that's the way
It was with Polly and me.
Dolina has told you that we had no right
To live in the Colony of the Sun;
But I believe I can convince you that we did.
It started simply enough.
I was telling Polly how a fellow had beaten me out
Of fifty bucks in a deal to sell horses in Laramie,
When she said, "Don't you remember how beautiful their hands were?"
I said, "Huh!" thinking she had snared a bottle somewhere.

152

"And the way we'd sit in the evening and they'd come down
To talk to us . . . all about the fun they had . . ."
"Fun? What fun? Where?"
"In the sky of course. And how nobody was ever hungry,
And no pawing over each other . . ."
"I know it was tough, honey, but . . ."
"And nobody ever called them names or made them cry."
"Sure. Sure thing. I'm beginning to remember . . .
Now that you mention it. All them fancy wings they had . . ."
"Wings? They didn't have any wings. They were just like
You and me . . . except they were so clean and happy . . .
Like . . . like . . ."
"Like angels maybe . . ?"
"Just like the sun! And it didn't matter to them
What anybody said . . ."
"Ah, honey . . . look now, don't cry. I'll get a good job
First thing in the morning. Then, soon as I'm on my feet,
We'll get hitched regular—just like other people—
And you'll have pretty dresses and get your hair fixed . . ."
"And you were always good to me when they were around.
You'd kiss me so soft, and your arms felt like
They wanted to tell me things just like they said . . .
How everybody could be good to a person . . .
But I don't care now!
I don't care!
Let them say anything . . . let them follow me in the street . . .
Let them whisper if they like . . . sure I'm not good enough . . .
Make fun of me . . . I know what you think . . . why don't you
Say it; That I'm sick, that nobody would want to touch me . . .
No, wait. Please. I didn't mean it. I'm tired.
I . . ."

You see how I lied to you.
I made up that Dolina stuff, and about the Colony.
I didn't know how to say it.
I could tell Polly, and she'd understand,
But it's too late for that now . . .
They've got poor Polly off in a cell on the hill,
And what she says to those sun-people of hers
Must be pretty hard for God to listen to.

NONE STAY THE WHITE SPEECH
OF HIS WANDERING

Where I shall be false to no one . . .
I rule not the least wingless bug
In this ingenuous clowndom . . .
And leapèd birds
Through paper air, while I measure
The eyebrows of a snothound. Because
I am standing in back of myself
With something very leaf and house
And

Dead. Life slopes upward at the angle
Of a wasp in a bear's nose, while I pile
My cities on top of rain and grass
And hills and dawns and crags and suns
And

Death. Because when you are very naked
You cannot clothe yourself with the partydress
Of state or church or opinion or of being
An article of merchandise on a country's
Bloodlist. You will confine yourself to The Kingdom.

TRIBUTE TO THE FLOWERS AND THE TOWNS AND T
ALL PEACEFUL MEN

Then there are beautifully definite

Beings in the air . . .

There are worlds

Above us . . .

Listen

O see the hand!

Kill. Burn.

In your night . . .

I bring a message

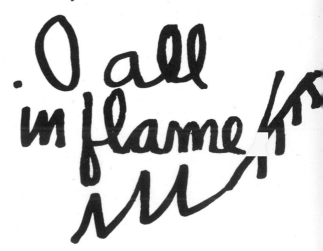

you will be still now

Sit down here and

Look at God

THE RICHES OF THE GENTLE PRINCE

I ever rule against the real. The panther is not attracted to the dove—save to eat him.
from 'The Book of the Wingèd Betrayal'

Town on the back of a hairy
Fish.

Lament. Fire creeps
Nearer.

Keep life.

Long heart in a red
Sky.

There grinds a world.
Blood . . . O all the deeps! The brightness
Grins.

Bang.
Look into my face.

World on the breast of a moaning
Creature.
I think it is mad.

Wipe the knife clean.
Make the sign of your kill.

THE CIRCLE OF APPARENT FATES

O all
in joy

The name! Appleman and sundeer . . . whitesoft cupboards
in a child'sroomdaddybigsky . . . Jesus! the damn horses
snorting fiery snot down on this land

The yellowclotted eyes of the war

O all every face bashed kicked bledgedmerryhell
into a wormy mess . . . But this is not dark. Or sad. An Adam
this way quick. See! It's pretty. Kind. To make you feel good.
To kiss that big stupid mouth of yours.

They're standing all around us.
"Nobody wants to kill anybody."
That's a lie from their start to your finish.
(Moo! I want to be milked. Said the damnfool cowworld.)

But the name is
and the name is Life

O all
in joy!

for over every man and over every thing the light O the beautiful
pure and dreadful Light

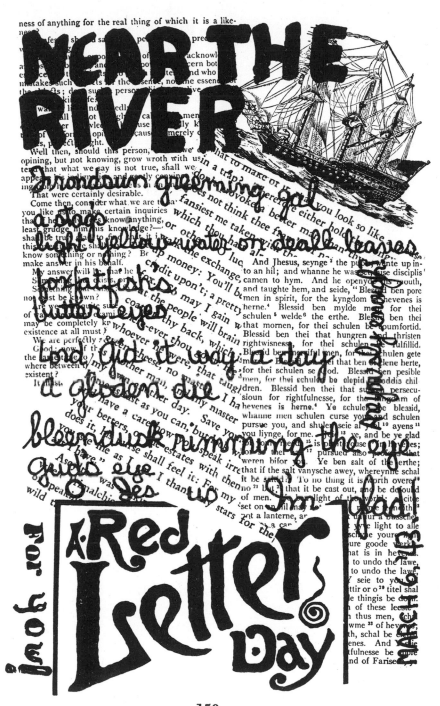

NEAR THE RIVER

A Red Letter Day

for you

SAYING ON A GRAY FIELD

Poor bent duster (a true hellman—no
Glitter near his mug.) . . . A red tree.
A red tree. A red tree.

Poor busted duster (lame lad of the icy
Night—no spinning to his brotherless
Dance.) . . . A blue wheel. A blue wheel.
A blue damn wheel.

See him there! Dustman, eh? O all that other
Bellyaching! It doesn't
Get you any sweet dolls. A real tribe.
A real tribe. A sonofabitch of a town.

Sometimes it's right.
The two cents get in. A red tree! Red tree!
O red wishalady tree . . .

THE SERPENT IS BEGINNING TO SING
ON THE DOORSTEP OF YOUR WORLD

Red heavy form
Of this glittering . . . rays of the river
Muddied by war. Tides of sleep
Falling back like blond flags
In the hands of a coffin
Where all may lie . . . Tumult
Of white.

Madness is white.
Shadow of the white panther.
Youth is white,
And their hate,
And their world.

The white anger.
Summer in a pit.
Bags of hair standing under God and
Laughing carelessly with bloody mouths.
Go down in it.
Let you be drawn in and rolled away
To dance before the White King.
He will kiss you.

THE BILLION FREEDOMS

Yes, then, always, as the rain, a star,
Or snow, the snow, snow,
Faces in the village, many dead on the roads
Of Europe, guns, go, yell, fall, O wait, what
Does life do, I know, knew, go mad, life goes
Mad, as the gentle rain, run, as the cold death
Comes into, into you, into the
Star-being man, is it quiet, quiet in the ground,
I grin, gunned silly, noble, is it noble to be part
Of, of the lie, it is a lie, war is, war is a lie,
What else is war, war is also a lie, love is not
A lie, love is greater, O love is greater
Than, war, wake my brothers, love is not a, lie,
Live, as the earth, as the, sun,
Stand in the beautiful, be, as the clean, full, fine,
Strong lives stood, hated, mocked, despised, drowned
In the sewers of poverty,
And in the sewers of the State, as Christ, was, for
He believed in life,
He believed in love, and in death, and war, and greed,
He did not believe, and any man who speaks
Of a Christian war, or of war as the savior
Of anything, that man is a liar, and
A, murderer, for no man can acquire position,
Or goods, or selfrighteousness
In a lie, except he be himself an enemy of truth,
And life, and God,
And a defiler in the temple of his kind, faces
In the villages of the world, millions dead

On the roads of Europe, what sin against reason
Is this, that they fought, fight, in a war
To save the evils
That cause war, for war is no evil
To those who have warred against the people,
And against truth, always, what crime
Against the soul of man is this, this fraud,
This mockery of life, that what is cheapest,
And dirtiest, and most debased, is thus smugly
Stamped on the forehead of, Christ, Who said,
Says, in the authority of God, thou shalt not
Kill, or take from another, O what are men
For, or God, now, as the light, and the good,
And the truth, and the love of one poor creature
For his fellow, fall, and the grandeur
Of mankind, like a blind snake,
Crawls, on its belly, into the slimy
Pit of oblivion, yes, then, always, as the rain,
A star, or as a fire burning forever in, all men.

DEPAFELIUSMOWKITBEYNAKILDEO

Father
The ice moves down
Over the earth
And golden
Heads
Bow in heaven
As the
S
   hag
      gy
Thing awakes
     to howl a t t h e c o l d m o o n

Father
What is theglory
And thelight
Does it smell nice
Are its ears soft
Are its eyes pretty
Could we crawl into its arms
And sleep and be warm
Would that be expensive
Would it cost as much
As we spend now
To get what we have here

Maybe the ice will tell us

THE TRIBES OF RAKALA

They prefer to sleep on tiny colored stones
Which are scattered over great golden mats
And glued down by pretty children
Who are grown for this purpose.
In the morning it may chance that wolves
Have eaten everybody, though this happens
But rarely now. However, the redder ones,
And those whose fins are most transparent,
Often scold each other; and the frozen heart
Bleeds its cold blood out over their land.

"To the hanging!" they sing; "O to the hanging
Near the throne of God!" What does that mean?
I ask them; but this leads me into trouble,
For they seem to resent all stupid questions.
So we begin to dig cities out of the ground,
And they show me how to build stars from webs
Of fire and I hitch trees to my cart and drive
Upon the enemies of life.
It is usually too light to see.
To the judgment! I shout; O to the judgment
Near the throne of God! "What do you mean?"
They ask me; and, taking the price-tags off heaven,
I put my arms around them—I advise my reader dear
To turn this page before I tell him what I mean

LIPS OF THE ANGEL

Hate the world
For the world is not love

Only life is loved
O only life is loved

Not the evil
Not the weak
Not the said thing
Not the saying of the Highest

Not the love of good at all
On the earth and off the earth

O only death is loved
Only death is the loved of every thing
On the earth and off the earth

WHAT IS THE BEAUTIFUL?

The narrowing line.
Walking on the burning ground.
The ledges of stone.
Owlfish wading near the horizon.
Unrest in the outer districts.

Pause.

And begin again.
Needles through the eye.
Bodies cracked open like nuts.
Must have a place.
Dog has a place.

Pause.

And begin again.
Tents in the sultry weather.
Rifles hate holds.
Who is right?
Was Christ?
Is it wrong to love all men?

Pause.

And begin again.
Contagion of murder.
But the small whip hits back.
This is my life, Caesar.
I think it is good to live.

Pause.

And begin again.
Perhaps the shapes will open.
Will flying fly?
Will singing have a song?
Will the shapes of evil fall?
Will the lives of men grow clean?
Will the power be for good?
Will the power of man find its sun?
Will the power of man flame as a sun?
Will the power of man turn against death?
Who is right?
Is war?

Pause.

And begin again.
A narrow line.
Walking on the beautiful ground.
A ledge of fire.
It would take little to be free.
That no man hate another man,
Because he is black;
Because he is yellow;
Because he is white;
Or because he is English;
Or German;
Or rich;
Or poor;
Because we are everyman.

Pause.

And begin again.
It would take little to be free.
That no man live at the expense of another.
Because no man can own what belongs to all.
Because no man can kill what all must use.
Because no man can lie when all are betrayed.
Because no man can hate when all are hated.

And begin again.
I know that the shapes will open.
Flying will fly, and singing will sing.
Because the only power of man is in good.
And all evil shall fail.
Because evil does not work,
Because the white man and the black man,
The Englishman and the German,
Are not real things.
They are only pictures of things.
Their shapes, like the shapes of the tree
And the flower, have no lives in names or signs;
They are their lives, and the real is in them.
And what is real shall have life always.

Pause.

I believe in the truth.
I believe that every good thought I have,
All men shall have.
I believe that what is best in me,
Shall be found in every man.
I believe that only the beautiful
Shall survive on the earth.

170

I believe that the perfect shape of everything
Has been prepared;
And, that we do not fit our own
Is of little consequence.
Man beckons to man on this terrible road.
I believe that we are going into the darkness now;
Hundreds of years will pass before the light
Shines over the world of all men . . .
And I am blinded by its splendor.

Pause.

And begin again

THE DIMENSIONS OF THE MORNING

Furtively sounding
In the high
Halls of God, the voice which is
Life begins to sing.
You will listen O you will not be afraid
To listen . . .
All these do:
The wolf, the fengy, the bear, the wide
Fish; and the deer, the silky rat, the snail,
The onises—even the goat
That waves his funny tail at trains
Is listening.
Do you now faintly
Hear the voice of life?
I will allow you respect for
Red apples and countries warm
With the races of men; peep over
The transom at China if you like;
But I will have no hatred or fear
Entering this poem.

It is big
Inside a man.
It is soft and beautiful
In him.
Water and the lands of the earth
Meet there.
I hand you a mountain.
I take the word Europe

Or the word death
And tear them into tiny pieces;
I scatter them at your feet.

Hand me a star.
Take me to a new city.
You are wasting your lives.
You are going along with your pockets
Full of trash.
You have been taught to want only the ugly
And the small;
You have been taught to hate what is clean
And of the star.
A dog will throw up
When he is sick;
Are you lower than dogs
That you keep it all down—
And cram more in?

The voice which is life
Shall sound over all the earth,
And over all who lie deep
In its green arms—
Go you to lie there as a fool, or as a child,
Tired from his beautiful playing,
To fall happily asleep?

SKY

HYDRAULIC

...the tombs of St. ...
...ers joined religious orders.
In the middle of the century ...
...gue which swept over ...
...the population. ... This is ...

...and it was called ...
...lague mentioned by Boccacc... ...
The 14th Century is called a transi... ...
the Renaissance had begun, but mediæval ideals ...
the new spirit in check. In 1302, the compass ...
...ented and was used by Columbus in 140... ...
...voyage of discovery. In 1319, paper was ...
...ade of rags. In 1320, gunpowder, which r... ...
...ionized the art of war, was invented. T... ...

rake

USIC KID?!

The evil that men do...

SPECIAL CIRCULAR TO SHAREHOLDER

Palm

for the kiddies

174

INSTRUCTIONS FOR ANGELS

Take the useful events
For your tall.
Red mouth.
Blue weather.
To hell with power and hate and war.

The mouth of a pretty girl . . .
The weather in the highest soul . . .
Put the tips of your fingers
On a baby man;
Teach him to be beautiful.
To hell with power and hate and war.

Tell God that we like
The rain, and snow, and flowers,
And trees, and all things gentle and clean
That have growth on the earth.
White winds.
Golden fields.
To hell with power and hate and war.

THE CONTINUAL MINISTRY OF THY ANGER

The kiss of loose-voiced reason . . .
Oil of heaven falling
On the sweat of towns . . .
What cold is,
Grass,
The ages of mankind, what gains light
And is a prey in my tusky sleep, what puts
Me at rage
Or to love
And to die.

Health to the lonely one,
Art in his teeth
Like a flaming star.
Death to the profane,
Who wears his art like a shoe
To take him into easier places.
For what the cold is, and grass, and men,
And to sleep, and to be angry, and to love,
And to die,
Artists do not know;
But art knows,
And is always waiting, and clean.

Make it Flying

flame flame flame flame flame flame flame flame flame
        flame
flame

Fill the dark.

        Do.

O move him sleeping

now the *flame*

Clean the earth.

Weep

It is

        I kiss Thee.

rotten little gray people

Now!

The rustle . . . He reaches upon you.

His mouth comes near

'O FIERY RIVER'

O fiery river
Flow out over the land.
Men have destroyed the roads of wonder,
And their cities squat like black toads
In the orchards of life.
Nothing is clean, or real, or as a girl,
Naked to love, or to be a man with.
The arts of this American land
Stink in the air of mountains;
What has made these men sick rats
That they find out every cheap hole?
How can these squeak of greatness?
Push your drugstore-culture into the sewer
With the rest of your creation.
The bell wasn't meant to toll for you.
Keep your filthy little hands off it.

O fiery river
Spread over this American land.
Drown out the falsity, the smug contempt
For what does not pay . . .
What would you pay Christ to die again?

ALL THIS IS MURDER

to thirst for the clean ! ! ! ! ! ! ! ! ! ! ! ! !

Born in fire

O what is the truth worth to anyone now . . . .

highest !

who will   FEED THE BLOODY PIGS OF WAR?

(under Christ's fiery tongue

the kindling of O the kindling of

wonderful creatures)

But all this is murder all this is murder

All this is murder all this is murder

All this is murder O all this is murder

The pigs of war fondle every living thing
And all this is the MURDER of human beings

'HOW SILENT ARE THE THINGS OF HEAVEN'

How silent are the things of heaven

The air must be kind
To the clouds and stars
That they never
Cry out
Or tear their lives away
From Thee
As we do
And have done

God, how silent are Thy fair children
That they never
Scream in fear
Or kill their sweet kind
In Thy name
As we do
And have forever done

O how silent are all heavenly things
And joyous in Thy white country
That they never howl
Like beasts in a bloody wood
As we do
And have done O Thou
Would go mad in the noise of this grave

THE CAUL, MUSIC OF THE SNOW, TRUTH IN KILISTOR'S DWELLING, AND THE STILL FIGURE I THE SNOW——AS A SIZE FOR HEAVEN

Pebble.
Birch.
Green wolf.
Destiny of Indians.
It is late blue cold bleeding.
Come in out of death, little creature.
It is love blown caught O love breaking the heart.

My head is covered with the bright caul of murder;
The music of the snow is heard by the dead,
And they are not comforted;
What is truth in the house of Kilistor
But a lie to slay all men?
And the still figure in the meadow
Has neither soul nor the light
To know God.

Mountain.
River.
Grim snare.
Delight of troops.
It is lost blind dark forever.
Come in out of the death, eternal being.
It is this huge beautiful life O life speaking out of the flame.

SADNESS OF THE HIGHEST BEING

It is not little he does
Whose life is of God.
His world has uses
In all men. As a flower,
Knowing the bright speech
Of the heavens,
Enjoys communion with light;
So will he be in us
The voice of our kingdom,
And a guide in this night.

O it is not evil he does
Whose life is of God.
His heart has uses
In every creature. As a mother,
Growing in strange height
The shape of her child,
Adds fingers to that fiery hand;
So will he be in us
A light for our kingdom,
And a sentinel in this fallen land.

'REST, HEART OF THE TIRED WORLD'

Rest, heart of the tired world.
Hush . . . go to sleep.
Men and cities keep their cold terrible watches,
And the ocean frets at these naked lands of pain.
O hushabye . . . and go to sleep.

This red rain . . .
To breathe . . .
To weep . . .
To love where only murder has been lain . . .
To find youth, and faith, and all their quick kin,
Buried deep in talking halls of horror . . .
No.
It is that we cannot see,
That we cannot hear,
That we cannot smell,
Or taste, or feel, or think;
For surely no will in heaven or earth
Could endure what we seem to possess;
We live in the shadow of a greater shadow—
But there is the sun!
And from him man shall have life,
And he shall have redress from the crimes
Of his most brutal habitation . . .

O rest, heart of the tired world.
Hush . . . and go to sleep.
There is a beautiful work for all men to do,
And we shall at last wake into the sun.

THE HOUSE OF THE SLEEPING EYE

Alike were death and the Medan graces
Of the folk who shone there . . . of whom
This: they were God's company.
"Shall we kiss the ladies in the cellar?"
This I asked. They counted me twelve times before
An old gubber said, "Those in the kitchen first,
Please. Life is too kind to waste on brassy fools."
I made a game with a crown that was lying
On a little pile of money at the feet of a green
Ape. I put all the money into a hole in the air,
And then howled at the ape, "O boil the grass and salt
The wedding, for the strength of travel renders flame
A bride." Sanin's daughters spread a pretty cloth
On the center table; a roast of eel was brought in;
Three scented falcon blew down from the ridgepole;
And then the old gubber sang, "I am a beautiful fellow.
See how my spirit glows in the light!" I struggled up
To a reclining position, and said, "There are four things
I must tell you:
The world is a dirty place.
Man's only talent is murder.
There is nothing whatever to have faith in.
I thank God that I live."
And then I set to work on the eel. The fine old gubber
Was snoring peacefully, his beard in a pitcher of cream.

C O N T E N T

CONTENTS

(Continued at back)

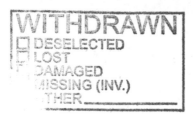

𝕌niversity of 𝕹ew 𝕭runswick
in 𝕾aint 𝕵ohn

Ward Chipman Library